MADE ACCORDING TO PATTERN

MADE ACCORDING TO PATTERN

*A Study of the Tabernacle
in the Wilderness*

by
Charles W. Slemming

*Author of:
These Are The Garments.
He Leadeth Me, Thus Shalt Thou Serve.*

CHRISTIAN LITERATURE CRUSADE
Fort Washington, Pennsylvania 19034

CHRISTIAN LITERATURE CRUSADE
Fort Washington, Pennsylvania 19034

CANADA
1440 Mackay Street, Montreal, Quebec

GREAT BRITAIN
The Dean, Alresford, Hampshire

AUSTRALIA
P.O. Box 91, Pennant Hills, N.S.W. 2120

First Edition 1938
Fourth Impression 1951
New and Revised Edition 1956
Reprinted 1964
First American Edition 1971
Reprinted 1974

SBN 87508-506-7

PREFACE

Of all the Old Testament studies, each holding its own attraction, and of all the typology, with its fascinating facets of truth, there is no subject that is more absorbing and no theme that is more complete in its truth than that of "the tabernacle."

It was back in 1928, when preaching at Faversham, that I saw the first model of a tabernacle and became interested. It was not long after when I found myself building my first model and beginning to study the subject. In the process of time the model was enlarged, and eventually I built three different models, had one created by an engineer, and then developed a very large flannelgraph.

1928 is a long time back, but over those thirty-five years this subject has never lost its interest; in fact, it becomes more fascinating, and when, from time to time, we take it as a series of studies or lectures, it always brings a great amount of blessing to the people, and it always grips my soul with a new sense of wonder and beauty as it reveals the Lord, the Church, and the will of the Lord concerning that Church.

It was in 1938 that, with a sense of inability and fear, I responded to the request of many people to put these lectures on the tabernacle into print, and thus it was that *Made According to Pattern* came onto the market. Even then one had no idea that the work would be accepted.

Therefore, it is with a rejoicing heart and thanksgiving to the Lord that I write this preface for the sixth edition. In doing so we can recommend the book with confidence, inasmuch as it is now registered as a standard work. It is being used as a textbook for students in a number of Bible colleges in the United States, and it has found its way into many countries around the world carrying blessing wherever it goes.

This edition of *Made According to Pattern* has been published in the popular paperback form to keep it in a price range which will enable it to have wider circulation.

Finally may we say that this book will bring the whole subject in a permanent form to many who have heard the lectures and seen the equipment, and, at the same time, we trust that many who might enjoy reading the book may in the future have the opportunity of attending some of the lectures and seeing the models.

So we prayerfully send out this edition, trusting that the Lord will put the seal of His blessing upon it.

Yours because His,

C. W. Slemming.

CONTENTS

LIST OF ILLUSTRATIONS

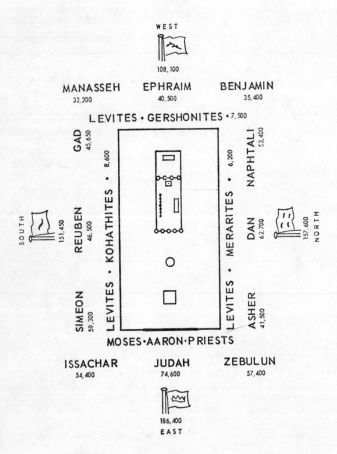

DIAGRAM 1.
PLAN OF THE ENCAMPMENT OF THE CHILDREN OF ISRAEL.

1

INTRODUCTION

Exodus 25:1-9. Exodus 35. Hebrews 8.

"And the Lord spake unto Moses, saying, Speak unto the children of Israel, that they bring me an offering: of every man that giveth it willingly with his heart ye shall take my offering. And this is the offering which ye shall take of them; gold, and silver, and brass, and blue, and purple, and scarlet, and fine linen, and goats' hair, and rams' skins dyed red, and badgers' skins, and shittim wood, oil for the-light, spices for anointing oil, and for sweet incense, onyx stones, and stones to be set in the ephod, and in the breastplate. And let them make me a sanctuary; that I may dwell among them. According to all that I shew thee, after the pattern of the tabernacle, and the pattern of all the instruments thereof, even so shall ye make it" (Ex. 25:1-9).

The Book of Exodus falls naturally into two distinct sections, the first being historical and the second legislative. Chapters 1 to 19 are occupied with the history of a people in bondage, the birth of a leader, their emancipation and journeyings as far as Sinai. Following these chapters come twenty-one more which outline the giving, and putting into action, of a threefold law, viz: moral, civil, and ceremonial. The moral law controlled individual life, the civil law governed national life, while the ceremonial law ordered religious life.

Concerning the book as a whole, but particularly in regard to the historical section, it has been recently asserted that outside evidence of Israel's stay in Egypt and of their journeyings in the wilderness is practically nil, and certainly very conflicting. But why need we get agitated as to how they crossed the Red Sea, and where? The fact is they did, or the Bible cannot be believed. Why argue the actual site of Sinai? Should we not be more concerned with the law given there, and the God who came there to dwell in the midst of a people whom He had chosen for Himself? The greatest blessing of the Word is found not so much in external evidence, although we thank God for it, but in internal and eternal truth appropriated with a simple faith in a Divine authorship.

It is certainly a romantic and thrilling story that we read in the introductory chapters, of God's great deliverance, but is it not a wonderful and inspiring continuation when, half-way through the book, God is desiring to dwell with them? Thus we come to the words of chapter 25:8: "And let them make *me* a sanctuary; that I may dwell among them." It is this tabernacle, with its priesthood and offerings, upon which we desire to meditate. This book will deal only with the tabernacle.

May we first be permitted to answer the critic, whom we meet so often, because in so doing we shall see our authority for spending so much time on this subject.

There are a large number of people who say these things have long since been done away with, but surely not so long since! For "beginning at Moses [the tabernacle, law, etc.] and all the prophets, *he* expounded unto them in *all* the scriptures the things concerning himself" (Lk. 24:27). Herein is our authority for studying these things now. Christ said that He was in them, so that we are neither rash, un-scriptural, nor out of date in dealing with Old Testament truths. Moreover, the importance of the subject can be readily seen when bearing in mind that "All scripture is given by inspiration of God, and is profitable for doctrine, for reproof, for correction, for instruction in righteousness" (2 Tim. 3:16). God only gave two chapters to the subject of the world's creation, chaos, and re-creation, or the generation, degeneration, and regeneration of the world, while He set apart no less than fifty chapters to this most entrancing subject under our consideration. If, then, God has inspired all for profit, He must have seen much more profit in the tabernacle than in the earth's early ages.

The allotment of these fifty chapters is:

Exodus . . . . . 13 chapters
Numbers . . . . 13 chapters
Leviticus . . . . 18 chapters
Deuteronomy . . . 2 chapters
Hebrews . . . . . 4 chapters, and other references.

Paul in his day made reference to the tabernacle.

People casually say, "Oh, they are only shadows." Have we a right to say "only" to anything in the purposes of God? True it is that they were shadows, but trace any shadow with the light before you and you will arrive at the substance; on the other hand, turn your back on the light and you will surely get away from the realities. What we purpose to do is to consider these shadows with the light of the Holy Ghost and Divine revelation before us until:

"The things of earth will grow strangely dim,
In the light of His glory and grace."

The first question we would ask ourselves is: "What is a tabernacle?" According to the dictionary it is "a temporary dwelling place." This may be interesting to trace out. God said, "Let them make *me* a sanctuary; that I may *dwell* among them" (Ex. 25:8). Was it temporary? Yes, just for 400 years, and then the temple which was for the time being, after which Christ took up His abode in the heart of the believer. "Know ye not that ye are the temple of God, and that the Spirit of God dwelleth in you?" (1 Cor. 3:16). Our body is likewise referred to as a tabernacle because it is the temporal abode of our soul. If we meditate upon the term "church" in the same way, we learn that it

is an *"ekklesia,"* meaning "that which is called out." The
church then is a community of people, and correctly the
word "church" should never be applied to a building. The
church is a called-out company of people who meet together
temporarily in a tabernacle until by and by they meet Him
to take up their abode with Him forever.

Another question often asked is: "Why was the tabernacle?" The same verse answers this question: "that I may
dwell among them." I once heard it said that the tabernacle
was a kindergarten lesson to teach an illiterate people something about God. It was not a lesson, it was a vital part
of their national life, and the people were not so illiterate.
They could show us how to build lastingly, and they practiced arts such as moderns cannot touch. Moses never built
a tabernacle and invited God to it, as this statement would
suggest; it was God who conceived the plan and instructed
man to build it because He had a desire to dwell among His
chosen people. This purpose of God thus to dwell develops
as we travel on through the Scriptures. The God who dwelt
in the tabernacle and the temple in the old dispensation
found an abode in Christ during His life on earth. "God
was in Christ, reconciling the world unto himself" (2 Cor.
5:19), and so He was called "Emmanuel...God with us"
(Matt. 1:23). Now in this present age He is abiding in us:
"Greater is he that is in you, than he that is in the world"
(1 Jn. 4:4b).

One final question: "How was the tabernacle?" This
question will take the rest of our studies to answer. Suffice
it here to say that it was "according to the pattern." It was
made according to the pattern of things in the heavenlies,
which things were revealed to Moses while in the mount.
It was, so it would appear, the pattern that was later shown
to John while he was on the Isle called Patmos, for we find
in the Revelation: an altar of sacrifice (Rev. 6:9); a sea
of glass (Rev. 4:6); seven golden candlesticks (Rev. 1:12);
the golden altar (Rev. 8:3); hidden manna (Rev. 2:17);
and the ark of His testament (Rev. 11:19). Repeatedly

in both Exodus and Hebrews the Lord said: "See that thou make it according to the pattern." God was very particular in planning it, no doubt Moses was in the building of it, and ought not we to be in the understanding of it? According to Exodus 31:1-3, God anointed Bezaleel with the Spirit of God for all manner of workmanship. He will also anoint us with the Holy Spirit for the true understanding and interpretation of these things. Every detail holds its spiritual significance and lesson, hence the carefulness.

It was made of the freewill offerings of the people. "Speak unto the children of Israel, that they bring me an offering: of every man that giveth it willingly with his heart ye shall take my offering" (Ex. 25:2). To this appeal the people responded so that the chosen workmen came to "Moses, saying, The people bring much more than enough for the service of the work, which the Lord commanded to make. And Moses gave commandment, and they caused it to be proclaimed throughout the camp, saying, Let neither man nor woman make any more work for the offering of the sanctuary. So the people were restrained from bringing. For the stuff they had was sufficient for all the work to make it, and too much" (Ex. 36:5-7). From whence did the delivered slaves get so much gold, silver, brass, spices, precious stones, etc.? We are told that they spoiled the Egyptians. God gave to them that they might give to God, and when the opportunity came they were not a whit behind in responding. Here lies our very first lesson, and a very important one too. Giving is a privilege, giving is a responsibility, giving is part of worship, but it must be given willingly, for the Lord loveth a *cheerful* giver. We are only stewards for God. If He has given to us, it is for the same purpose that we might give to Him.

It was a giving that left no one out. Gold, silver, spices, precious stones, came from the rich; blue, purple, scarlet, brass, from another class; goats' hair from the poor. For those who had not substance, there was the giving of skill and labor. This, too, was varied. Woodworkers, metalworkers, weavers and embroiderers, all had a share in the great work. So it is in the work of the Lord today. We can all of us play our part, remembering one thing. When He gave, He gave His best, He gave His all, He held no reserve. Lord, help us to do the same.

"What shall I bring to the Saviour?
What shall I lay at His feet?
I have no glittering jewels
Gold, or frankincense so sweet.

"Gifts to the Saviour I'm bringing,
Love's richest treasure to lay
Low at His feet with rejoicing
Ere yonder sunset today.

"What shall I bring to the Saviour?
Lips His dear praises to sing,
Feet that will walk in the pathway
Leading to Jesus, our King.

"What shall I bring to the Saviour?
Love that is purest and best,
Life in its sweetness and beauty,
All for His service so blest."

2

FELLOWSHIP OF THE TABERNACLE

Have you ever asked yourself the question: "Why did God create me?" Such questions are good because they provoke thought; thought demands investigation, and investigation should drive us to the Word of God. The great purpose for which God created man was that He might have fellowship with him.

This thought, like many others, is conveyed right through the Bible. Most of the great themes of doctrine find their birth in the early chapters of Scripture and their full consummation in the closing chapters. In this subject of fellowship we learn that God not only desires it but constantly moves nearer to the heart of man. Strangely enough man is not so anxious to have fellowship with God as God longs for it with man.

With this in mind we learn that the tabernacle is but one cog in the wheel of communion, one movement in the opening of the beautiful flower of fellowship, one place of residence in a series of dwelling places.

1. God In The Garden. "And they heard the voice of the Lord God walking in the garden in the cool of the day..." (<u>Gen. 3:8</u>). The God who made man and placed him in the garden was the God who came down to that man, walked with him, and talked to him. We are not told how long this fellowship continued. Possibly a long time, until the day arrived when God came to Adam but Adam did not come to God. Instead, Adam tried to hide from God,

19

a thing man cannot do. What had happened? Sin had come into the heart of man, that sin which separated man from God; but be it known that, while sin had broken that fellowship, it had not altered the desire of God for it, not for a moment of time. Man may turn his back, but with God there is no shadow of turning. We find, therefore, that God sought to establish that fellowship wherever and whenever the opportunity afforded. He walked with Enoch, He talked to Abram, He communed with Moses and others, until we find

2. God In The Tabernacle. And the Lord spake unto Moses saying, "Let them make me a sanctuary; that I may dwell among them" (Ex. 25:8). It is to be observed that the narrative does not suggest that Moses proposed building a tabernacle and then inviting God to occupy it, but contrariwise. God, who had looked down in love and pity upon these people and had brought them out of the bondage of Egypt and was then leading them toward a promised land, desired not only to direct them but to "dwell" with them. Therefore, He instructed Moses to build this tabernacle and to set it up in the midst of the camp, just as a Bedouin chieftain would have his tent pitched in the midst of his encampment. The tabernacle, as we shall learn, was a portable, temporary dwelling place. These people were pilgrims living in tents, moving from place to place. The idea of the tabernacle, therefore, was that God had become a pilgrim with pilgrims and occupied a "tent" with tent-dwellers — or, God came right down to where man was that He might have fellowship with him. "There I will meet with thee, and I will commune with thee . . ." (Ex. 25:22).

3. God In Solomon's Temple. "So that the priests could not stand to minister because of the cloud: for the glory of the Lord had filled the house of the Lord" (1 Kings 8:11). The pages of history tell of the ending of the pilgrimage, of the people entering the land of Palestine, and then occupying it. Pilgrimage gives place to residency, wanderings to settlement, desert to fruitful fields, and tents to houses. They were now an established people. They had become a kingdom. They had a King.

It was then that David observed that, while he dwelt in a house of cedar, God still dwelt in curtains (the tabernacle). David's request was that he should build a house worthy of His God. While God appreciated David's desire, yet He could not permit David to build such a temple because he was a man of war. Nonetheless God gave His consent, but it was to be David's son who would build that temple. So Solomon came to the throne, and with great magnificence and with tremendous costliness he built the temple. Then on the great day of dedication the glory of the Lord came down and filled the place.

God was now in the midst of His people occupying a permanent house in the midst of a permanent people. Here God and man met in fellowship and communion. In this place man could pray and God has promised to hear. Thus God was in the midst of His people. Both the tabernacle and the temple were wonderful in their detail and structure. The one was a portable building, the other a permanent structure.

After many years man again turned his back upon God. He was serving other gods having given himself to idolatry. God's anger was kindled against him, so that Nebuchadnezzar, King of Babylon, came up against Jerusalem and destroyed it. The temple was demolished. The furniture, the gold, and the brass were carried away and the people became exiles in a strange country. This is known as the Babylonian Captivity.

After seventy years there was a return of the people under the hands of Ezra and Nehemiah.

4. God In Zerubbabel's Temple. "And this house was finished . . . . and the children of Israel . . . kept the dedication of this house of God with joy" (Ezra 6:15, 16). This temple was poor and insignificant compared with the one built by Solomon, so much so that "many of the priests and Levites and chief of the fathers, who were ancient men, that had seen the first house, when the foundation of this house was laid before their eyes, wept with a loud voice" (Ezra 3:12). Poor as this building was by comparison, yet God was pleased to receive it and to take up His abode with His people again. God only accepts the best, and He accepted this because it was the best the nation could offer Him seeing they were an impoverished people who had only just returned from exile. God looked on the outward appearance, and accepted it only as it was in a right relationship with desire, longing, and ability.

From the Old Testament one moves to the New Testament and is soon introduced to

5. Herod's Temple. But God was not in this temple. As the Bible does not give an account of the building, it is necessary to turn to history. From these pages it is learned that Herod suggested that the Jewish people should give him the right to replace the temple, built by Zerubbabel, by another which he would build, and which would be more worthy of the name of their God and of their worship. This suggestion became a fact.

It is known that Herod was a wicked man and a cruel king. He had no religion in him and no interest in the Jewish people. Thus the question is raised — Why did Herod want to build this temple? The answer is that Herod knew that he was a much hated man, and that when death came he would soon be forgotten, as the Scripture says: "For there shall be no reward to the evil man; the candle of the wicked shall be put out" (Prov. 24:20). Therefore he conceived the idea of building a temple for the perpetuation of his name — and in this he succeeded. If this be true, then Herod's Temple was not in the will of God.

This thought can be strengthened by the fact that in Herod's Temple there was no Ark of the Covenant and no Shekinah glory. Jesus only ministered in the outer court. He had no access to the inner sanctuaries. God was not there. It had been made to become a den of thieves in the hardness and coldness of its ritualism.

Someone will say: "Did not Jesus refer to it as His Father's house?" What the Lord said was: "My [Father's] house shall be called the house of prayer, but ye have made it a den of thieves." He stated what it should be, but obviously it was not. This corruption could have dated back to the time when Herod, with wrong motive, built the temple.

The reason why God was not in this temple was because it was not in His will. He had never required its construction. He had fellowshiped with man through the offerings and the sacrifices of the temple of the Old Testament, but God is moving away from ritual to reality, from shadow to substance, and had at this time provided His own temple, for

6. God Was In Christ. "To wit, that God was in Christ, reconciling the world unto himself, not imputing their trespasses unto them..." (2 Cor. 5:19). "Jesus answered and said unto them, Destroy this temple, and in three days I will raise it up. But he spake of the temple of his body" (John 2:19, 21).

His name was Immanuel, which means God with us. In the person of Christ, in the form of man, God was getting nearer to man in fellowship. While forms and ceremonies remained cold and inflexible, Jesus was moved with compassion. He had feelings and understanding. He was tempted in all points as we are. We have said that God only occupies the best — here was a sinless life, here was the perfect Man.

Each temple was short-lived. The tabernacle wore out and was substituted by the temple. Solomon's Temple was destroyed by Nebuchadnezzar. Zerubbabel's Temple was destroyed by Herod. Herod's Temple was destroyed by Titus. The temple of Christ's body was destroyed by the Romans when they nailed It to a tree.

Now another temple comes into being.

7. God In You. "Know ye not that ye are the temple of God, and that the Spirit of God dwelleth in you?" (1 Cor.

3:16). "For ye are the temple of the living God; as God
hath said, I will dwell in them, and walk in them; and I will
be their God, and they shall be my people" (2 Cor. 6:16b).
"Christst in you, the hope of glory" (Col. 1:27b). If this
be true — and it is — then our bodies should be kept sweet
and clean, and pure and holy. The realization that our
bodies are the temples of God should remove from our
hearts and minds all doubtful and questionable things, for
God only dwells in the best. Oh, the wonder of this truth!

God has surely come very near to man when He takes up
an occupancy within us. Meditate on it, beloved! It should
lead to a life of full surrender and of holiness.

But God can only occupy our bodies for a limited time
because these bodies are subject to death. This temple will
be destroyed by the last enemy which is death.

This leads us right into the full consummation of this
fellowship.

8. God With Man And Man With God. "For we know
that if our earthly house of this tabernacle were dissolved,
we have a building of God, an house not made with hands,
eternal in the heavens" (2 Cor. 5:1). This is the only
temple which is eternal. It knows no end.

We started with God coming down to earth to fellowship
with man. We end with man going up to God in heaven
to dwell with Him for evermore.

> "Forever with the Lord,
>   Amen, so let it be.
>   Life from the dead is in that word,
>   'Tis immortality.
>   Here in the body pent,
>   Absent from Him I roam,
>   Yet nightly pitch my moving tent
>   A day's march nearer home."

3

RELATIVE POSITIONS

Exodus 26. 18-22. Numbers 2 and 3.

"And the Lord spake unto Moses and unto Aaron, saying, Every man of the children of Israel shall pitch by his own standard, with the ensign of their father's house: far off about the tabernacle of the congregation shall they pitch. And on the east side toward the rising of the sun shall they of the standard of the camp of Judah pitch throughout their armies. . . . And those that do pitch next unto him shall be the tribe of Issachar: . . . Then the tribe of Zebulun: . . . On the south side shall be the standard of the camp of Reuben according to their armies: . . . And those which pitch by him shall be the tribe of Simeon: . . . Then the tribe of Gad: . . . Then the tabernacle of the congregation shall set forward with the camp of the Levites in the midst of the camp: as they encamp, so shall they set forward, every man in his place by their standards. On the west side shall be the standard of the camp of Ephraim according to their armies. . . . And by him shall be the tribe of Manasseh: . . . Then the tribe of Benjamin: . . . The standard of the camp of Dan shall be on the north side by their armies: . . . And those that encamp by him shall be the tribe of Asher: . . . Then the tribe of Napthali: . . . These are those which were numbered of the children of Israel by the house of their fathers: all those that were numbered of the camps throughout their hosts were six hundred thousand and three thousand and five hundred and fifty. But the Levites were not numbered among the children of Israel; as the Lord commanded Moses. And the children of Israel did according to all that the Lord commanded Moses; so they pitched by their standards, and so they set forward, every one after their families, according to the house of their fathers" (Num. 2.).

There are several interesting and instructive things to be gained by meditating upon the position of the tabernacle and the furniture, and of the general relationship, whether stationary or on the move.

1.   Its Relation To The Camp.   The tabernacle always found its position in the very midst of the camp. You will notice by diagram 1* exactly how the various tribes were arranged. The tents were pitched at a distance from the building. Judah, with Issachar and Zebulun, on the east numbered 186,400 men. On the south was the encampment of Reuben, Simeon, and Gad, under the standard of Reuben, numbering 151,450 men. At the back of the tabernacle, westward, was Ephraim, together with his associates Manasseh and Benjamin. They totalled 108,100 men. To the north was Dan, accompanied by Asher and Naphtali, making another 157,600 men, thus bringing the totality of men of twenty years and upwards to 603,550, not including the tribe of Levi. This tribe, divided into four families, pitched between the tabernacle and the camp, a family on each side. 8,600 of the family of Kohath occupied the south side. The Gershonites were on the west, in number 7,500, and on the north were the Merarites, another 6,200. On the front, or east, were the tents of the fourth family, Moses the leader, Aaron the High Priest, and the sons of Aaron, the priests. Then right in the center was God.

God is, and always has been, the God of order. God never did mean man to please himself. Christ did not do so. He came to do His Father's will. The apostle said, "Though he were a Son, yet learned he obedience by the things which he suffered" (Heb. 5:8). It is the desire of the Lord that we submit to His plans and purposes, "You

* See page 12.

in your small corner and I in mine." By obedience to this plan, we should certainly find the Christian life a far, far happier one.

The significance and beauty of this arrangement is better understood if we were to consider a Bedouin company moving about the desert. Every camp has its sheik or chieftain. We see him leading the way on his camel or Arab steed, and carrying in his hand his spear, which varies from fifteen to twenty feet in length. When the chieftain wanted to settle his camp for a while he would just plant his spear into the ground. That was the sign of rest. His servants would immediately erect their master's tent behind the spear and then pitch their own tents around in a circle or circles according to the size of the camp. The sheik then dwelt in the midst of his people. When he desired to move on, he removed his spear and rode forth. So we see the picture. A company of about a million and a half people wandering through the wilderness. Their chieftain is Jehovah God, whose spear is a pillar of cloud and fire. When it moves they move — when it stays they stay. His servants, the Levites, pitch their Master's tent (the tabernacle) while the host pitch around. What a joy to move when God moves, and to stay when God wishes. This is to be in the center of His will, and God in the midst of us.

One more thought just here. Was not this scene in the mind of the psalmist when he wrote, "He that dwelleth in the secret place of the most High shall abide under the shadow of the Almighty" (Ps. 91)? No enemy, whoever he might be, could touch anyone who had been invited by a sheik into his tent. It was a place of safety. Praise God, we have been brought into His pavilion, and His banner over us is love.

2. Its Relation To Heaven. Boards on the north! Boards on the south! ! Boards on the west! ! ! That means the entrance on the east; or, in other words, the tabernacle in the wilderness always faced east. It looked toward the sunrising. This is, or should be, the attitude of the church.

Her outlook should be eastward, toward the sunrising from whence the Lord will make His appearance: "For as the lightning cometh out of the east, and shineth even unto the west; so shall also the coming of the Son of man be" (Mt. 24:27).

Remembering again that the Old Testament types are "a shadow of good things to come, and *not the very image* of the things..." (Heb. 10:1), the suggestion is not that we should have our places of worship facing east or west, but that our hearts should ever be toward the coming of the Lord. Thus it is that the hope of the coming of the Lo' becomes a purifying hope.

3.   Position Of The Furniture.   Just a word about the position of the furniture, this was not left to the discretion of Moses any more than was the building.

God said exactly where it should be.   Just inside the gate was the brazen altar; between the altar and the tabernacle, the laver; these both were in the court.   Inside the sanctuary on the south side stood the candlestick, and on the north side the table of shewbread.   Before the veil the altar of incense stood and beyond the veil the ark of the covenant.

Now look at Diagram 3*.   Was it chance?   No!   All things are written for our learning, and here we see the whole tabernacle stamped with the Cross.   Look at it again.   The foot of the Cross is in the place of suffering and death — the altar of burnt offering.   The head of it is within the veil in the place of glory — the *Shekinah* of a finished work. From without to within a straight road via salvation, sanctification, intercession, and a rent veil into the presence of the Lord.   On the right hand and on the left the arms hold out two choice blessings — fellowship at the table and unity of testimony in the golden candlestick.

4.   Position While Journeying.   There is one further truth on the subject of position.   Our thoughts have only been on the stationary aspect.   Let us look at the order of

* See page 30.

things when moving. Diagram 2 will enable us to see that order at a glance. The three tribes that were before the tabernacle moved forward under the standard of Judah. Judah means the "Praise of Jehovah." God always puts praise first, and the praising man always finds himself in the forefront of victory. The Gershonites removed, folded, and packed onto two wagons all the fabrics — curtains, coverings, hangings of the court, gate, and door, while the family of the Merarites, who were responsible for the structural part of the building, dismantled and packed onto four wagons the boards, bars, pillars, and silver sockets of the tabernacle; also the brass sockets, pillars, pins, and cords of the court. These all moved next. The tribes under Reuben's standard fell in behind these wagons. This brings us to the center of the procession, and here was the family of the Kohathites bearing their sacred charge — the furniture, the ark covered by the veil and badgers' skins, and then an outer covering of blue cloth. The covering of the furniture was done by Aaron and his sons. The table of shewbread was covered with a blue cloth, upon which were laid the dishes, spoons, bowls, and covers — also the bread. Over all this was a cloth of scarlet, then badgers' skins. The candlestick came next, also covered with a blue cloth and seemingly placed into a bag of badgers' skins through which was put a bar in order to carry the candlestick. The golden altar was likewise covered with a blue cloth and badgers' skins. The vessels of the sanctuary are next mentioned as being put into a blue cloth, covered with badgers' skins and carried on a bar. These would include the many unnamed things as oil vessels. Finally came the brazen altar. This was covered with a purple cloth upon which were placed

| PILLAR OF CLOUD | — (God leads the way)

JUDAH
Issachar
Zebulun
GERSHONITES
with
two wagon carrying the
CURTAINS, COVERINGS, HANGINGS, GATE, and DOOR.
MERARITES
with
four wagons carrying the
BOARDS, BARS, PILLARS, SOCKETS, COURT PILLARS,
COURT SOCKETS, PINS, and CORDS.
REUBEN
Simeon
Gad
KOHATHITES
bearing the

| ARK | — (God in the midst)

TABLE
CANDLESTICK
ALTAR
ALTAR
(LAVER?)
EPHRAIM
Manasseh
Benjamin
DAN
Asher
Naphtali

DIAGRAM 2.   POSITION WHEN JOURNEYING.

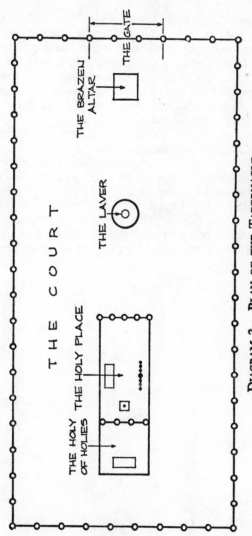

THE GATE

THE BRAZEN ALTAR

THE LAVER

THE COURT

THE HOLY PLACE

THE HOLY OF HOLIES

Diagram 3. Plan of the Tabernacle.

the censers, fleshhooks, shovels, basins, etc. All was covered with badgers' skins. No mention is made of the laver. Whether it is because it was not covered one cannot say, but it must have been there. It is interesting to note the variation of color and order of these coverings, all having a divine purpose. Along with the Kohathites was Eleazer, the son of Aaron, who was responsible for the lighting oil, anointing oil, incense and meal, etc.

These holy vessels were followed by the standard of Ephraim and his confederates, while Dan, with Asher and Naphtali, came up as a rearguard. God, therefore, led the way in journeyings in the pillar of cloud, yet remained in His rightful place in their midst.

God has a task for each of us to perform, one responsibility differing from another. We must not cover another man's calling, but see to it that we faithfully discharge our own. Thus will the work of the Lord make steady progress.

4

GENERAL CONSTRUCTION

Exodus 25, 26, 27, 30, 36, 37, 38, and 40.
Hebrews 9.

"Then verily the first covenant had also ordinances of divine service, and a worldly sanctuary. For there was a tabernacle made; the first, wherein was the candlestick, and the table, and the shewbread; which is called the sanctuary. And after the second veil, the tabernacle which is called the Holiest of all; which had the golden censer, and the ark of the covenant overlaid round about with gold, wherein was the golden pot that had manna, and Aaron's rod that budded, and the tables of the covenant; and over it the cherubims of glory shadowing the mercyseat; of which we cannot now speak particularly. Now when these things were thus ordained, the priests went always into the first tabernacle, accomplishing the service of God. But into the second went the high priest alone once every year, not without blood, which he offered for himself, and for the errors of the people: The Holy Ghost this signifying, that the way into the holiest of all was not yet made manifest, while as the first tabernacle was yet standing: which was a figure for the time then present, in which were offered both gifts and sacrifices, that could not make him that did the service perfect, as pertaining to the conscience; which stood only in meats and drinks, and divers washings, and carnal ordinances, imposed on them until the time of reformation. But Christ being come an high priest of good things to come, by a greater and more perfect tabernacle, not made with hands, that is to say, not of this building; neither by the blood of goats and calves, but by his own blood he entered in once into the holy place, having obtained eternal redemption for us. For if the blood of bulls and of goats, and the ashes of an heifer sprinkling the unclean, sanctifieth to the purifying of the flesh: how much more shall the blood of Christ, who through the eternal Spirit offered himself without spot to God, purge your conscience from dead works to serve the living God? . . . Moreover he sprinkled with blood both the tabernacle, and all the vesels of the ministry. And almost all things are by the law purged with blood; and without shedding of blood is no remission. It was therefore necessary that the patterns of things in the heavens should be purified with these; but the heavenly things themselves with better sacrifices than these" (Heb. 9:1-14, 21-23).

Before taking a general survey of the whole structure, it is important to note that God began where we purpose ending, at the Ark of the Covenant. We shall make our approach to it along the path of God's providing, from without to within. But when God laid that path it was from within to without. Notice how striking the narrative is. "And let them make me a sanctuary; that I may dwell among them. According to all that I shew thee, after the pattern of the tabernacle, and the pattern of all the instruments thereof, even so shall ye make it. And they shall make an ark . . ." (Ex. 25:8-10). Man would erect his building, after which he would consider the furniture; but here, before God says one word about the building design, He describes minutely a piece of the furniture. What was the position of this Ark of the Covenant? It was in the holy of holies, or in the center of things, and everything else then adjusts itself. Is that not how God deals with man? The first great principle runs: "Is thine heart right with God?" Dear reader, if your heart is not according to the divine plan, nothing else will be, and the whole teaching of the tabernacle will fail in its appeal, neither can you adjust your life to its many lessons.

Now let us take a general look at the construction of the

tabernacle because, if we do not, we lose much. Many of the errors abroad today, and much of the "wrongly divided" Word, are due to failure to scan the whole horizon of divine truth, or the whole subject as a subject before scrutinizing minutely. We cannot discuss the full use and purpose of a stamen until we have a general idea and knowledge of flowers, botany, and bees; nor could we explain the actual results of the functioning of a carburetor and why it is in one certain place unless we have surveyed generally the whole theory of a gasoline engine. Even so with God's great truths; know the purposes of God and you will know the detail of His work. Let us see the tabernacle as a whole first, then we shall understand the component parts.

The Court. The building itself stood in a courtyard formed by a surround of 280 cubits (according to Wilkinson, the cubit as found in the Nilometer of Elephantine is 20.625 inches, and as found in the wooden Egyptian cubits it is also 20.625 inches) of fine twined linen, to which were added twenty more cubits of the same worked in blue, purple, and scarlet, which formed the gate. This material, five cubits in width, hung upon sixty pillars which were so placed as to form a perfect oblong one hundred cubits long and fifty cubits wide, with the gate at one end. The foundation of this court consisted of sixty sockets of brass buried into the ground, or sand, into which the pillars were inserted. Each one of these pillars was finished off at the top with a cap called in the Scriptures a chapiter, which was overlaid with silver. A silver connecting bar, or fillet, held the pillars at an equal distance apart, while the curtains were attached by means of silver hooks. All was secured by cords and brass tent pegs.

The Tabernacle itself was the building standing within and toward one end of the court. It comprised forty-eight boards, each ten cubits high and one and a half cubits wide, having two tenons or feet. These were inserted into ninety-six silver sockets, each weighing approximately 125 lbs. or 6 tons as an estimated total. The boards were united together by fifteen bars, five on each side and five on the west end. These bars passed through a series of rings which were in the boards. Five pillars set into sockets of brass, and upholding a door of blue, purple, and scarlet and fine twined linen, made the front, or the east end of the building. A veil of the same size and materials, embroidered with cherubim, and hanging on four pillars set into sockets of silver, made a partition between the only two rooms the tabernacle contained, viz: the holy place twenty cubits long, and the holy of holies, a perfect cube of ten cubits.

One thing remains to complete the structural part and that is the roof. This took the form of two sets of curtains and two sets of coverings. The first and innermost set consisted of ten curtains made of blue, purple, scarlet and fine twined linen with cherubim and fastened together. Its overall dimensions were forty-two feet by sixty feet.

Over and above this were eleven curtains of goats' hair. These too were joined, and totaled forty-five feet by sixty-six feet.

The first set of coverings was rams' skins dyed red, and the last or outer, badgers' skins.

It now remains to look briefly at the furniture. In the court there were two pieces of brass, or of wood overlaid with brass; three pieces in the holy place of gold, or of wood overlaid with gold; and only one piece stood in the holy of holies. Its value was not in brass or gold, but in the blood that was sprinkled on the mercy seat.

Passing through the gate of the court, we are at once confronted with the first and the largest piece of furniture — the brazen altar. Five cubits square and three cubits high, it was the great place of sacrifice. Around this the people congregated bringing their various offerings. Halfway between the altar of burnt offering and the tabernacle was the brazen laver, the place of washing for the officiating priests. We are tempted to pause and comment on these things, but we shall, in due course, deal fully with every part. Entering now into the sacred building we are almost startled with the amazing contrast. Everything is gold and silver, all scintillating in the flickering lights of the seven-branched candlestick, a mass of beautiful ornamental work, all of it typical in one way or another. This stands to the left as we enter. Opposite, on the right, is the table of shewbread overlaid with gold, and having upon it the twelve loaves of shewbread. Right opposite us is the third article, with its ever burning fire, the golden altar of incense. Can we go beyond that veil which hangs with imposing awe and dignity behind the golden altar? Not then, but we can now for the veil has been rent. If we could have entered, what a sight would have met our eyes! There, in solitary grandeur, rested the Ark of the Covenant, with its beautiful cherubim, and its blood sprinkled mercy seat under which were secreted the two tables of testimony, Aaron's rod that budded, and the golden pot of manna, while above the mercy seat was the glory of the *Shekinah* presence of God.

Let us come out and glance at the building again. One very conspicuous thing we have not mentioned: it is the pillar of cloud, the outward evidence of the inward presence of Jehovah God. It was their guide and their guard.

In the general construction one cannot help but notice that a large number of the measurements are multiples of fives:

THE COURT

60 pillars	. . .	12	x 5
60 chapiters	. .	12	x 5
60 sockets	. . .	12	x 5
120 pins	. . .	24	x 5
100 cubits long	.	20	x 5
50 cubits wide	.	10	x 5
5 cubits high	.	1	x 5

THE TABERNACLE

30 cubits long	.	6	x 5
10 cubits wide	.	2	x 5
10 cubits high	.	2	x 5
100 silver sockets	20	x 5
15 bars	. . .	3	x 5
5 bars each side	1	x 5
10 curtains	. .	2	x 5
50 taches	. . .	10	x 5
100 blue loops	.	20	x 5

THE ENTRANCES

Gate	20 cubits wide	4	x 5
„	5 cubits high	1	x 5
Door	10 cubits wide	2	x 5
„	10 cubits high	2	x 5
„	on 5 pillars	1	x 5
Veil	10 cubits wide	2	x 5
„	10 cubits high	2	x 5

HOLY OF HOLIES

10 x 10 x 10 cubits   2 x 5

BRAZEN ALTAR

5 x 5 cubits	. . .	1	x 5
5 vessels	. . . .	1	x 5
5 animals	. . .	1	x 5
5 offerings	. . .	1	x 5

IN THE ARK

10 commandments   2 x 5

HOLY PLACE

20 cubits long	. . . .	4	x 5
10 cubits wide	. . . .	2	x 5
10 cubits high	. . . .	2	x 5

What does this all mean? Five is the number of grace, as seen in such instances as the feeding of 5,000 people with five barley loaves, a wonderful act of grace on the part of the Lord; and when David took five stones from the brook he revealed that he was depending on the "unmerited favor" (grace) of the Lord God. In the Church of God it is grace everywhere, "all of grace," abounding grace — and blue is found everywhere in the tabernacle, covering the furniture, and on the high priest.

One word as to its value. It has been estimated from Exodus 38:24-31, in the following terms:

	Talents	Shekels	
Gold	29	730	$877,300
Silver	100	1,775	195,136
Brass	70	2,400	690
			$1,073,126

Adding to this the cost of wood, fabrics, priestly garments, precious stones for the breastplate, etc., one and a quarter million dollars would be a reasonable estimate, without labor.

5

SILVER SOCKETS

Exodus 30:11-16. Exodus 38:25-28. Matthew 17:24-27.
1 Peter 1:18, 19.

"And the Lord spake unto Moses, saying, When thou takest the sum of the children of Israel after their number, then shall they give every man a ransom for his soul unto the Lord, when thou numberest them; that there be no plague among them, when thou numberest them. This they shall give, every one that passeth among them that are numbered, half a shekel after the shekel of the sanctuary: (a shekel is twenty gerahs:) an half shekel shall be the offering of the Lord. Every one that passeth among them that are numbered, from twenty years old and above, shall give an offering unto the Lord. The rich shall not give more, and the poor shall not give less than half a shekel, when they give an offering unto the Lord, to make an atonement for your souls. And thou shalt take the atonement money of the children of Israel, and shalt appoint it for the service of the tabernacle of the congregation; that it may be a memorial unto the children of Israel before the Lord, to make an atonement for your souls" (Ex. 30:11-16).

"And the silver of them that were numbered of the congregation was an hundred talents, and a thousand seven hundred and three-score and fifteen shekels, after the shekel of the sanctuary: A bekah for every man, that is, half a shekel, after the shekel of the sanctuary, for every one that went to be numbered, from twenty years old and upward, for six hundred thousand and three thousand and five hundred and fifty men. And of the hundred talents of silver were cast the sockets of the sanctuary, and the sockets of the vail; an hundred sockets of the hundred talents, a talent for a socket. And of the thousand seven hundred seventy and five shekels he made hooks for the pillars, and overlaid their chapiters, and filleted them" (Ex. 38:25-28).

Reference has already been made to the effect that all the material was the freewill offering of a willing people. There was one exception with which we will deal here. God had instructed that, when the men of twenty years of age and upwards were numbered for the army, they should pay an amount in silver as a ransom for their souls. This appears to be a strange action, especially so when we see the reason, "that there be no plague among them" (Ex. 30:12). If they had paid a levy or tax, one might have passed it over; but why a ransom? Why should numbering cause a plague? God had not forbidden the numbering of Israel at this time, or at any rate no prohibition is recorded. Was it not that He knew the heart of man that it was full of pride, a pride that would possibly tend to depend on numbers rather than on God, a pride that "always goeth before a fall"; and so He demanded from them, at the time of numbering, a piece of silver. It was called a ransom, and as such reminded the man being enlisted into the army of Israel, which was the army of God, that he himself was unworthy of such a calling. It is also called "atonement money," "atonement" meaning "to cover." His sin, therefore, was covered before he committed it. In other words, it was God's merciful provision against the sins of His people. But surely there is no covering for sin apart from shed blood? That is so — but the Lord is laying a foundation in type, and silver is the price of life. Men were bought and sold for silver. We remember Joseph who was sold for twenty pieces of silver, and the Lord Jesus Christ whose life was covenanted for thirty pieces of silver. Similarly it was in the payment of half a shekel that the men of Israel were delivered from the visitation of a plague. It is well to point out here the difference between "atonement" and "redemption," because Christ is often referred to as atoning for sin. He never did. Only once does the word occur in the New Testament, i.e., Romans 5:11b: "By whom we have now received the atonement." The Greek word is *katallage* and is translated everywhere else "reconciliation" or "reconciling." To "atone" means to "cover." That is what laws and offerings did, but they did not erase. "For what the law could not do, in that it was weak through the flesh, God sending his own Son in the likeness of sinful flesh, and for sin, condemned sin in the flesh" (Rom. 8:3). Christ's work was to redeem, or to set us free from the power of sin and death.

Half a shekel after the shekel of the sanctuary was what each man paid. It weighed a quarter of an ounce and, at five shillings an ounce, was equal to thirty-one cents. "The rich shall not give more, and the poor shall not give less," each man shall pay for himself. God fixed the price and man must comply. There was no question of personal opinion. How like salvation! God has laid down His conditions. It is faith in Christ, whether we be high or low, rich or poor, learned or ignorant, prince or pauper, black or white, young or old. The condition is simple, it is within the reach of all — faith in Christ.

Six hundred and three thousand five hundred and fifty men was the result of the numbering, each paying his ransom money. This naturally brought in a good revenue, totaling three hundred and one thousand seven hundred and seventy-five shekels of silver. The Lord had specified how the accumulated silver was to be utilized. It was "for the work of the ministry" and for the making of silver sockets as a foundation for the tabernacle. Three thousand shekels went to a talent so there were a hundred sockets each weighing a talent of 125 lbs. apiece. Ninety-six of these were to make foundations for the boards, and the other four as sockets for the pillars of the veil. This foundation of more than six tons of silver was necessary because of Israel's being in the wilderness, and the Lord said that a man who built his house upon sand was foolish; sand is unstable. Are not the ideas, theories, and doctrines of men ever changing? They cannot be relied upon and so we need a foundation for our faith which is solid, dependable, and lasting. That basis is found in redemption that is in Christ Jesus and His death.

The foundation of the church in the wilderness, then, was the price of atonement; similarly, the Church of the New Testament is resting entirely on Christ's redemptive work.

Of the balance of one thousand seven hundred and seventy-five shekels, part was used to form silver fillets or connecting bars and hooks; also it was used for the overlaying of the chapiters. Further reference will be made to these in the chapter on the court.

May not the Apostle Peter have had the tabernacle in his mind when he wrote his first epistle, and from it drawn out a spiritual application when he said, "Forasmuch as ye know that ye were not redeemed with corruptible things, as silver and gold, from your vain conversation received by tradition from your fathers; but with the precious blood of Christ, as of a lamb without blemish and without spot" (1 Pet. 1:18, 19)?

There is a very interesting connection between the New Testament and the Old with regard to this ransom money. It is to be found in Matthew 17:24-27: "And when they were come to Capernaum, they that received tribute money came to Peter, and said, Doth not your master pay tribute? He saith, Yes. And when he was come into the house, Jesus prevented him, saying, What thinkest thou, Simon? of whom do the kings of the earth take custom or tribute? of their own children, or of strangers? Peter saith unto him, Of strangers. Jesus saith unto him, Then are the children free. Notwithstanding, lest we should offend them, go thou to the sea, and cast an hook, and take up the fish that first cometh up; and when thou hast opened his mouth, thou shalt find a piece of money: that take, and give unto them for me and thee."

The tribute money here referred to was not a national tax

imposed by a ruler. That was demanded without question. This tribute was a custom which came into vogue as a result of the ransom money paid in Exodus 30. In acknowledgment of God's goodness all men of twenty years of age and upwards paid annually of their own free will the amount of half a shekel of the sanctuary, as a contribution towards the maintenance of the temple and the temple of worship. It was, therefore, a kind of church rate. The collectors of this money came on this occasion to Peter asking (not demanding) "Doth not your master pay tribute?" Peter, in his impetuous manner, seems to answer up without any thought or consideration. "Yes," and then enters the house evidently to appeal to the Lord, but the Lord prevents him from speaking by appealing to Peter first with a question: "What thinkest thou, Simon? of whom do the kings of the earth take custom or tribute? of their own children, or of strangers?" Peter was caught. The truth was manifest. Peter had answered wrongly. The members of a royal family were always exempt from paying taxes. The Lord draws a comparison between Himself, the King of kins, and an earthly king. He had claimed that He was the Son of God. If this tribute was for the upkeep of God's house, then God's Son was exempt — "Then are the children free." Then in the Lord's usual gracious way, as Peter had said, "Yes," and as the people might misconstrue Christ's action, He, not willing to cause offence, said to Peter "Go thou to the sea, and cast an hook, and take up the fish that first cometh up; and when thou hast opened his mouth, thou shalt find a piece of money. . . ." The fact that the fish had a piece of money in its mouth was not the miracle. The Rev. L. T. Pearson points out in his book *Through the Holy Land* that, among the many species of fish found in the Sea of Galilee is one called the *"musht,"* commonly known as "Peter's fish." "The male," says Mr. Pearson, "has a habit of carrying the young in its mouth, and of sucking them in in time of danger. Sometimes it will carry a stone or other obstacle to keep the young out. The *'musht'* has been found to have other obstacles than stones in its mouth. They are attracted by bright objects and even coins have been picked up by them."

Wherein lies the miracle then? Firstly, the Lord said, "Take up the *first* fish." Seeing that there are some forty or more species of fish in the Sea of Galilee, it could have been any other of these; and secondly, "when thou hast opened his mouth, thou shalt find a piece of money." The margin says, "A stater." It is half an ounce of silver, about sixty-four cents in value. That is double the amount paid by the men of Israel in Exodus 38:26. "And give . . . for me and thee." The Lord paid for Peter as well as for Himself. Since then He has paid the price of redemption for all men in the giving of Himself, and the shedding of His blood. Oh! glorious foundation of the Church of Christ.

6

THE BOARDS AND BARS

Exodus 26:15-29.   Exodus 36:20-34

"And thou shalt make boards for the tabernacle of shittim wood standing up.   Ten cubits shall be the length of a board, and a cubit and a half shall be the breadth of one board.   Two tenons shall there be in one board, set in order one against another: thus shalt thou make for all the boards of the tabernacle.   And thou shalt make the boards for the tabernacle, twenty boards on the south side southward.   And thou shalt make forty sockets of silver under the twenty boards; two sockets under one board for his two tenons, and two sockets under another board for his two tenons.   And for the second side of the tabernacle on the north side there shall be twenty boards: And their forty sockets of silver; two sockets under one board, and two sockets under another board.   And for the sides of the tabernacle westward thou shalt make six boards.   And two boards shalt thou make for the corners of the tabernacle in the two sides.   And they shall be coupled together beneath, and they shall be coupled together above the head of it unto one ring: thus shall it be for them both; they shall be for the two corners.   And they shall be eight boards, and their sockets of silver, sixteen sockets; two sockets under one board, and two sockets under another board.   And thou shalt make bars of shittim wood; five for the boards of the one side of the tabernacle.   And five bars for the boards of the other side of the tabernacle, and five bars for the boards of the side of the tabernacle, for the two sides westward.   And the middle bar in the midst of the boards shall reach from end to end. And thou shalt overlay the boards with gold, and make their rings of gold for places for the bars: and thou shalt overlay the bars with gold" (Ex. 26:15-29).

"And thou shalt make boards for the tabernacle of shittim wood standing up." The last two words of that statement are rather impressive — "standing up." Are you, Christian reader, standing up? Many are sitting at ease, others are reclining in indolence — but let us consider the matter.

In the previous chapter we dealt with the silver sockets as a type of the redemptive work of the Lord Jesus Christ by whose blood the foundation of the true Church has been laid. These boards, standing on such a foundation and forming the dwelling place of God, must naturally turn our thoughts to the believers, the living stones of God's temple who rest upon the finished work of the Cross.

Shall we look first at the characteristics revealed in the boards.

1. They Were Made Of Shittim Wood. The acacia tree, from whence such wood comes, is a native of the Sinaitic Peninsula and the desert. There was a time when we, who are now the saints of God, were strangers to His grace. We grew in the world and drew from the world's barrenness that which met the needs of our life. In such a condition we were never truly happy nor satisfied.

2. These Trees Were Cut Down. Saul of Tarsus was one of these trees. While on his way to Damascus he was met by God and was cut down to the earth. Do not we remember when the Spirit of God cut across our lives and laid us low causing us to say, "Lord, what wilt Thou have me to do?" This means a severance from the old life, our link with the earth broken.

3. The Trees Were Then Cut Up. This was a very necessary thing because the natural condition of the acacia tree is knots and twists. There is nothing straight about it and it is, therefore, of little or no use for building purposes unless trimmed. What an outstanding type of the believer! How we do need to be straightened, and oh! how we object sometimes. The work of the Spirit is a continous one. So many feel they have all when they receive salvation, but that is far from true. There is development, shaping into Christlike character, a daily growing in grace and in knowledge of Christ Jesus the Lord. The sap of selfishness must be dried out, the knots of hardness must be smoothed down to gentleness and compassion and the twists of half-heartedness must be straightened for they will never make for a perfect fitting and a unity in the Spirit in which the Lord always delights to dwell. The boards, having thus been prepared so far as their natural condition was concerned, were then overlaid, and thus beautified, with pure gold. How suggestive! remembering that wood is a type of humanity, and gold of Divinity because of its imperishableness. God not only works in the natural man and transforms the human nature, but He also clothes us with His own Divine nature. Peter tells us that we "might be partakes of the divine nature" (2 Pet. 1:4).

So much for the nature of the boards; now a word as to their shape. Each of the forty-eight boards was ten cubits high and a cubit and a half in width. The thickness is not stated. On the face of each board there were rings through which bars were passed. Each board had at the lower extremity two tenons, or two feet, to allow it to stand solidly on its foundation. The mention of two tenons carries our thoughts back to the Scripture quoted at the head of this chapter, "And thou shalt make boards for the tabernacle of shittim wood *standing up.*" All tents were erected by *driving in* the stakes and pins. Their existence was dependent on a grip of the desert. But to these boards were given two feet, and for them were provided two sockets, so that they stood independent of the sand of the desert. They just stood upright *in* the desert and not *of* it. Once they, as trees, were well rooted into it. What separated the boards from the sand? silver — a ransom price. You, dear reader, if Christ's, are not your own. You, too, should be *in* the world but not *of* it, separated through the blood of Christ. "Come out from among them, and be ye separate, saith the Lord, and touch not the unclean thing . . ." (2 Cor. 6:17). Are you among those who say, "It is difficult to stand"? May we remind you that God has given you two feet and two silver sockets. There are so many Christians who have one foot established in the "redemption that is in Christ Jesus," but they have the other foot in something else — pleasure for one, politics for another, socialism for yet a third, while a fourth is always concerned about the various "isms" abroad. We would not condemn some of these things if in their rightful place, but when they are put on a par with Christian living, so as to cause one's testimony and faith to be weakened, then stability is lost.

While these boards have no relationship with the desert, they certainly have with each other and with God. First note their union with each other. Forty-eight boards, 10 x 1½ cubits, stood so "fitly framed together" as to become one building. They all stood as it were shoulder to shoulder with such a unity that daylight could not be seen between them. There was no rubbing nor chafing because they were so well-balanced. All this was resultant upon an equal foundation. It is when believers are out fundamentally that they are out with each other. One leaning toward this theory and another toward that dogma means a loss of unity and fellowship into which the Enemy of souls enters and splits the work, or else he causes a chafing which creates an irritability that brings discord and discontent. Not only were the boards "compacted by that which every joint supplieth" (Eph. 4:16) but they were equal in their height, forty-eight boards ten cubits high. How practical is the teaching of the tabernacle! Solomon said that "Jealousy is cruel as the grave" (Song 8:6). It has ruined many a man, but God would have us learn from the evenness of height that there is no room nor place in the church for one to look down upon, or despise, another, or to be jealous of another. We must follow the inspired exhortation of the Apostle Paul who said, "Let each esteem other better than themselves" (Phil. 2:3b). Let us reach "unto a perfect man, unto the measure of the stature of the fulness of Christ" (Eph. 4:13b).

Secondly, their relationship to God must be considered. "Twenty boards southward . . . twenty boards northward . . . and eight boards westward" means that the tabernacle always faced eastward, that is toward the sunrising. The suggestion is that this building always looked toward God. In any case, this should certainly be the attitude of the church of the present day. We should, as we pass through this night of sorrow, keep our eyes toward daybreak — the east — for when the Sun of Righteousnes shall appear shadows will flee away:

> "Turn your eyes upon Jesus,
> Look full in His wonderful face,
> And the things of earth will grow strangely dim
> In the light of His glory and grace."

The two corner boards have caused much concern as to what they were or how they were fastened. The writer, having built several models of the tabernacle, has met this problem from the practical viewpoint, as also that of the unstated board thickness. It is to be noted that nothing is said of the complete measurement of the tabernacle length, viz: thirty cubits. Commentators and others have calculated it from twenty boards each a cubit and a half broad. If this were the complete length then one cannot put inside it a holy ot holies 10 x 10 cubits and a holy place 20 x 10 cubits (these measurements must be inside — one never measures rooms from the outside), because there must be a deduction for the thickness of the back boards, together with the thickness of the pillars of the veil and those which supported the front door. The outer measurement must, therefore, be increased, and the text allows for it in the two corner boards. In the Hebrew the word "corner" here is *mequtsoth,* meaning "angle." Now take a board, cut it down the center on a miter, reverse one piece and join the two pieces together again and you have a "corner" or "angle" board in the two sides.

In this way the corner boards would add two half cubits to the six boards, making the required ten cubits for the width; also it would increase the total length by half a cubit. This would allow the pillars of the veil to be half a cubit in diameter. The thickness of the boards, back and sides, would be adjusted in the miter cut. The rooms will then be found fitting according to the prescribed measurements. The top and bottom of these corner boards fitted into a ring. Thus the whole was strengthened and locked. Has not the Word of God told us that Jesus Christ is the chief cornerstone, the source of strength and stability for all believers?

Into each board were put presumably three rings through which the bars were to pass. Some have suggested that the three rings are a type of the triune blessing, the grace of the Lord Jesus, the love of God, and the fellowship of the Holy Spirit. Others say that they represent faith, hope, and charity, and still others suggest that they point to the work of the Triune God on the behalf of each believer. All are good, but the writer prefers the latter, because it is so encouraging to be reminded that Father, Son, and Spirit are working for and on our behalf. We can find the three statements all in one chapter — Romans 8: "What shall we then say to these things, if *God be for us,* who can be against us?" (ver. 31). "Who is he that condemneth? It is *Christ* that died, yea rather, that is risen again, who is even at the right hand of God, who also maketh intercession *for us*" (ver. 34.) "Likewise the Spirit also helpeth our infirmities: for we know not what we should pray for as we ought: but the *Spirit* itself maketh intercession *for us* with groanings which cannot be uttered" (ver. 26).

Silver sockets kept the boards from sinking into the sand or losing equality of height. Their close relationship with each other prevented a tilting to the right or left. One thing remained, they could lean backwards or forwards and so get out of line and touch with each other but for a yet further provision made by the Lord. "Thou shalt make bars for the boards and overlay them with pure gold." These bars consolidated the whole into one. There were five bars on each of the sides north, south, and west. The center bar went from end to end and the other four were apparently half lengths, two above and two below the center one. There are many who teach us that the center bar was invisible and was made to go through the inside of the boards. Might we spend a few moments considering this, as its position makes a difference to its interpretation. Was it logically and mechanically possible? If it were possible, it was most improbable. Each board was approximately 17 ft. 6 in. high and 31½ in. wide. What was the thickness? Twenty boards of this width stood side by side, therefore the bar that shot through from end to end was at least fifty-two feet long. What thickness would that bar have to be not to snap? Having estimated your measurements could you get your bar through the inside of your boards, and having put it in could you withdraw it? Remember, the bar was not metal nor bamboo, but shittim wood overlaid with gold. I cannot imagine that your measurements, whatever you have estimated them to be, will allow for this, and even if they do, were you to bore a large enough hole right through the center of such a board, you would have robbed it of its strength, and a wind, or even the weight of the expanse of curtains and coverings, would snap the board completely in two. Further, those who give expression to an "invisible bar" in typifying the subject, refer to the bars as representing the Trinity of the Godhead — Father, Son, and Holy Spirit — stating that the center bar speaks of the Holy Spirit because He is invisible. Two errors are obvious in this method of interpretation. Firstly, only three bars are referred to, while Scripture speaks of five; and secondly, surely God the Father and God the Son are as invisible to the human eye as God the Holy Ghost!

Enough for the negative side, but let us now think on the positive side. (1) "Thou shalt make rings for the bars," not for some of the bars. (2) "And the middle bar in the midst of the boards." 8 ft. 9 in. from the top and 8 ft. 9 in. from the bottom is surely in the midst of the boards. The difficult statement of Exodus 36:33, can be harmonized with this because, while it says "shoot through" it does not say "inside."

An illustration will help just here. A car skids on the road and shoots through the crowd of people which is standing on the corner. Does that car go through the inside of each individual? Of course not! The illustration is self-explanatory.

Now that we see five bars all passing similarly through rings around the outside of the boards binding them together into one complete structure, we come to the more important thing. What do they teach us? The Apostle Paul tells us that God has given five gifts of ministry to the Church; they are found in Ephesians 4:11: "And he gave some, apostles; and some, prophets; and some, evangelists; and some, pastors and teachers." These bars and ministries are readily harmonized. The first two ministries are represented by the two lower bars — "And are built upon the foundation of the apostles and prophets . . ." (Eph. 2:20). This, of course, does not mean that Peter, Paul, and others are the foundation of our faith. The foundation is lower than the bars and is definitely Christ's redemptive work. It means that apostles and prophets were the substructure of ministry while ours is part of the superstructure. The center bar, reaching from end to end, would remind us of the center ministry stated, that of the evangelist. What an extensive work is his; how far-reaching! "Go ye into *all* the world, and preach the gospel to *every creature*" (Mark 16:15). The evangelist having done his part, then come the labors of the pastor and teacher, one to shepherd and care for the flock, and the other to instruct them in divine things and so ever seek to lift them higher and higher. These two ministries are typified by the two top bars. To say that these bars thus speak of church ministry is no speculation, for if we read on in Ephesians 4, "comparing spiritual things with spiritual," we shall find that both the bars and the gifts were given for a similar purpose, "For the perfecting of the saints, for the work of the ministry, for the edifying of the body of Christ: till we all come in the unity of the faith, and of the knowledge of the Son of God, unto a perfect man, unto the measure of the stature of the fulness of Christ: that we henceforth be no more children, tossed to and fro, and carried about with every wind of doctrine, by the sleight of men, and cunning craftiness, whereby they lie in wait to deceive; but speaking the truth in love, may grow up into him in all things, which is the head, even Christ: from whom the whole body fitly joined together and compacted by that which every joint supplieth, according to the effectual working in the measure of every part, maketh increase of the body unto the edifying of itself in love" (Eph. 4:12-16).

Taking away the bars from the boards would mean that a broadside wind would scatter the boards like ninepins, and the whole structure would collapse. Likewise if we had not this God-given ministry in the church, every wind of doctrine would scatter the flock, but God has not only established the church in the present dispensation, but He also has supplied the means of consolidation. Therefore, "touch not the Lord's anointed" and despise not the ministry.

Still writing to the Ephesians the apostle draws yet another comparison between the tabernacle of the Old Testament and the church of the New Testament. "In whom all the building fitly framed together groweth unto an holy temple in the Lord: in whom ye also are builded together for an habitation of God through the Spirit" (Eph. 2:21, 22).

The tabernacle was a habitation of God in wood and gold. The church is a habitation of God in spiritual and living stones.

7

THE CURTAINS AND COVERINGS

Exodus 26:1-14. Exodus 36:8-19.

"Moreover thou shalt make the tabernacle with ten curtains of fine twined linen, and blue, and purple, and scarlet: with cherubims of cunning work shalt thou make them. The length of one curtain shall be eight and twenty cubits, and the breadth of one curtain four cubits: and every one of the curtains shall have one measure. The five curtains shall be coupled together one to another; and other five curtains shall be coupled one to another. And thou shalt make loops of blue upon the edge of the one curtain from the selvedge in the coupling; and likewise shalt thou make in the uttermost edge of another curtain, in the coupling of the second. Fifty loops shalt thou make in the one curtain, and fifty loops shalt thou make in the edge of the curtain that is in the coupling of the second; that the loops may take hold one of another. And thou shalt make fifty taches of gold, and couple the curtains together with the taches: and it shall be one tabernacle. And thou shalt make curtains of goats' hair to be a covering upon the tabernacle: eleven curtains shalt thou make. The length of one curtain shall be thirty cubits, and the breadth of one curtain four cubits: and the eleven curtains shall be all of one measure. And thou shalt couple five curtains by themselves, and six curtains by themselves, and shalt double the sixth curtain in the forefront of the tabernacle. And thou shalt make fifty loops on the edge of the one curtain that is outmost in the coupling, and fifty loops in the edge of the curtain which coupleth the second.

And thou shalt make fifty taches of brass, and put the taches into the loops, and couple the tent together, that it may be one. And the remnant that remaineth of the curtains of the tent, the half curtain that remaineth, shall hang over the backside of the tabernacle. And a cubit on the one side, and a cubit on the other side of that which remaineth in the length of the curtains of the tent, it shall hang over the sides of the tabernacle on this side and on that side, to cover it. And thou shalt make a covering for the tent of rams' skins dyed red, and a covering above of badgers' skins" (Ex. 26:1-14).

The curtains and the coverings, in other words the roof of the tabernacle, will complete the structure except for the pillars of the door and of the veil. There are two sets of curtains and two sets of coverings. We will not deal with these in the same order in which they are recorded in Exodus 26, viz: from inside to outside, because that is God's order. He plans from within the sanctuary — we approach from without.

In each instance we shall observe that they teach us something about the Christ. So we see Him as the "foundation," "chief cornerstone" and "top stone" of the Church, or Christ as our all, and in all.

First Covering — Badgers' Skins. One verse is all that we have to record both the covering of badgers' skins and the rams' skins. As to whether the animal referred to as a badger belonged to the land or the sea is difficult to ascertain; the latter appears more likely. At any rate, the badger that we know in the west was an unknown animal in the Sinaitic Peninsula. The only other reference in the Scriptures is in Ezekiel 16:10, where we read, "and shod thee with badgers' skins." We conclude, therefore, that they were skins of a preservative nature used as a protection for that which was beneath from the outward elements of storm, rain, sand, or scorching sun. It must have been a weather-beaten skin with no beauty or attractiveness. This skin would be practically all that could be seen by the onlooker.

Here then is our first picture of Christ. He has become the covering of all those who put their trust in Him. The wrath, which was our due, fell upon Him, the storm cloud of judgment broke upon His Head, the scorching sun of infernal hatred spent its rays upon His Body. "He was despised and rejected of men; a man of sorrows and acquainted with grief," until it was said of Him, "[He is] as a root out of a dry ground: he hath no form nor comeliness; and when we shall see him, there is no beauty that we should desire him." What does the world see in Jesus today? Nothing. Why? Because it does not know Him, but we do. Because we were not content to look upon such a marred form without seeking to find out the reason for such suffering. Our eyes, by grace, pierced the badger skin of the human frame and beheld the rams' skins which showed us both the reason and the motive.

Second Covering — Rams' Skins Dyed Red. The ram is found to be the animal of substitution, through its taking the place of another, as seen in the story of Abraham and Isaac, and in certain of the offerings. It is also the animal used for the consecration of the priesthood and is spoken of as the "ram of consecrations" in Exodus 29 and Leviticus 8. Cannot we link these two truths together in Christ as we see Him consecrating Himself to the work of the Cross that He might become our substitute? I should have died, but He died for me, as the ram did for Isaac. Skins (we are not told of what animal) were used in the garden of Eden as a substitute for the fig leaves of man's providing.

We proceed a little deeper toward the interior and meet with the two sets of curtains. It is very important to note that the first set of curtains was always called the "ohel" or tent of the congregation, and the second the "mishkan" or tabernacle; so that the tabernacle was not the tent, and the tent was not the tabernacle. The tabernacle was inside the tent, and the tent covered the tabernacle. The tabernacle was God's dwelling place. The tent was man's meeting place.

First Curtain — Goats' Hair. It comprised a set of eleven curtains, each thirty cubits long and four cubits wide. Joined together it formed one great tent, thirty cubits by forty-four cubits, covering the tabernacle in its entirety.

Of what were these curtains made? Goats' hair. What was their color? Black. Just here many people make a big mistake. They describe these curtains, whether by picture or word, as white and as representing the righteousness of Christ. They conclude this because goats' hair is white in the western world; but the tabernacle was built in a country where a white goat is a rarity — eastern goats are black. This, of course, completely reverses the spiritual application propounded by many. Before proceeding further let us consider two references in Scripture which reveal to us that goats' hair is black, bearing in mind that all tents in the East are made of goats' hair and are spoken of by the Bedouin as their "home of hair." Turn to the Song of Solomon 1:5: "I am black, but comely, O ye daughters of Jerusalem, as the tents of Kedar, as the curtains of Solomon." Now read carefully the story of Jacob and Laban. Both were cunning and crafty men, both were always out for personal advantage, both sought to outwit the other when the opportunity afforded itself. These two schemers were found bargaining in Genesis 30:25-43. Jacob proposed to Laban that he should have all the speckled, spotted, and ringstraked goats. In other words, all that were other than black. If, in the natural course of events, these were in the majority we could not imagine a man of Laban's wily character agreeing. But in verse 34, Laban said, "Behold, I would it might be according to thy word." This surely is sufficient evidence that the goats were naturally black; then it was that Jacob began his plan to get the better of his uncle. By putting whitened sticks before the watering troughs of the goats that were with young he mesmerised them, causing them to bring forth their young in an unnatural way, hence they were born ringstraked, speckled, and spotted, and he won the better of the bargain.

Remembering what has already been remarked about the difference between the *"ohel"* and the *"mishkan,"* we see that God in the tabernacle appointed that He should dwell within the "house of hair" as Israel did. What a foreview of "Immanuel" — "God with us," or God in Christ Jesus dwelling in the same human form in which we find ourselves. It has been said that an eastern shepherd wears a sheepskin coat because he thinks the sheep like to see him as one of them. The idea may be sentimental, but the ideal is seen in Jesus, "For verily he took not on him the nature of angels; but he took on him the seed of Abraham. Wherefore in all things it behoved him to be made like unto his brethren, that he might be a merciful and faithful high priest in things pertaining to God . . ." (Heb. 2:16, 17).

A word further concerning the color of these curtains. As has already been intimated, their color being black instead of white we must necessarily change the usual interpretation. Instead of the suggested righteousness, we see Christ as the sin offering. We shall note that this interpretation brings a beautiful harmony, firstly with the general teaching of Scripture concerning the goat, for the goat is a type of sin:

A kid of the goats was the sin offering animal (Lev. 9:3).

Two goats were used on the day of atonement (Lev. 16: 5-28).

Sheep and goats represent saved and unsaved nations (Matt. 25:32).

Christ came in the likeness of sinful flesh (Rom. 8:3).

Also we use black as the emblematic color of sin.

Secondly, this interpretation is in harmony with the general teaching of the curtains and coverings, for all three outer fabrics speak of Christ's suffering — badgers' skins, the despised One — rams' skins, the substitute through death — goats' hair, the sin offering. These all bring us to the inner beauty seen in the fourth curtain, and in His perfect life, and thus it was that He brought "many sons to glory."

Now a word concerning the number of curtains used.

There were eleven of them, sewn together in five and in six, and then the two pieces were united by fifty brass taches laying hold of one hundred loops, fifty loops being in each of the two selvedges. We shall say more about these taches later, as there are others in the next set of curtains. Eleven, we are told, is the number of disorganization. Two illustrations of this number will explain:

1. When Joseph told his dream of eleven stars doing obeisance to him, he offended his brethren who, as a result, sold the dreamer and so brought disorganization to the family (Gen. 37).
2. The betrayal of Christ by Judas resulted in his leaving the twelve, and from the Passover Feast to Pentecost it was always the "eleven." During this period everything was disorganized so far as the disciples were concerned.

Christ, as the sin offering, certainly disorganized the work of the Enemy and put him to flight. Ten curtains we find just covered the tabernacle, the eleventh, or the sixth as it is called in verse nine (showing which way round it was placed) was to be doubled in the forefront. When the coverings were put into position, they covered all the curtains except this one thus hanging; so that Israel saw one-eleventh of the goats' hair curtain exhibited while the ten-elevenths remained unseen by man. Looking into the life of Christ we very soon see the meaning of it all. Christ spent approximately thirty-three years on this earth, that is eleven threes. Ten elevenths of this life, which is thirty years, were spent in secret except the incident at the age of twelve when He, as a Jewish boy, arrived at His coming-of-age, and so was brought to the temple. Then, at the age of thirty John said: "Behold" and pointed the people to "the Lamb of God, which taketh away the sin of the world," and so, for the last eleventh of His life, in a three-year ministry, He was revealed to the world — as what? the sin offering, as John declared Him to be. No wonder the Emmaus disciples said their heart burned within them as He taught them from Moses and the prophets. Surely these things cause our hearts also to burn and our souls to rejoice. It is behind the work of Calvary and beyond the sacrifice of a great sin offering that all spiritual blessing lies. What are we going to find as we take yet another step into the:

Second Curtain — Fine Twined Linen. This set of curtains is always called the *"mishkan"* and is translated "the tabernacle," thus called because it was actually the roof without which the building is not a true house. It comprised ten curtains each twenty-eight cubits by four cubits. They were sewn together in two sets of five joined by one hundred blue loops taking hold of each other and fifty golden taches, making the total dimensions of twenty-eight cubits by forty cubits. The whole of the fabric was worked in blue, purple, and scarlet as well as the fine twined linen, with a design of cherubim. Have you noticed that the colors are always mentioned in the same order? Blue, purple, and scarlet — purple is the harmonizing color that brings the other two together. Much can be said concerning these three colors and their significance, but we shall content ourselves with a bare outline here and will touch the subject again. These colors are to be seen also at the gate, the door, the veil, and the high priest's ephod.

Blue. This is a heavenly color, and is always associated with the blue sky. It is the emblematic color of divinity and grace. We will only think of the divinity aspect now. Look up into the beautiful blue vaulted heavens — how impressive, how serene! Sometimes clouds come between and temporarily blot out the sky, but they never pollute it. It is high above all the clouds, mists, and fogs. Nothing can pierce the heavens, nor even reach them. What is man's journey to the moon when we remember that it is only 238,000 miles from the earth, while the sun is 93,000,000 miles away. Also light, traveling at 186,000 miles per second, takes four years to come from the nearest fixed star. So is the divinity of Christ. Man gets into his "higher

critical balloon" and propounds some modern conception
of God and Christ, but how foolish. Christ is divine; who
can approach such a subject? Let them blot the view with
their clouds of doubt and their mists of modernism, what of
it? The clouds will disperse, "moderns" will disappear,
but He remaineth. Remember, dear reader, even when,
because of clouds, you cannot see Him, He remains. The
heavens are illimitable, unchangeable, and eternal. So is
Christ in His great uncreated glory and unfathomable divinity. One holds the pen of a ready writer when writing
concerning Him. Enough to say that blue in these curtains
typifies Jesus as the divine Son of God.

Scarlet. We bring the third color under observation next,
rather contrary to scriptural order but for reasons readily
seen when we deal with the purple. If we were in Palestine,
"the land of the Book," we should appreciate the significance
of this color more because it is the color of the Palestinian
earth. Turning then from blue to red, we drop our eyes
from heaven to earth. Adam, the name given to man in
Genesis, comes from the root word meaning "red earth."
Adam, the first man, was of the earth earthy. Jesus was
the second man, the Lord from heaven.

Another beautiful illustration of this truth is to be found
in Genesis 25:25: "And the first came out red, all over
like an hairy garment; and they called his name Esau."
Esau, then, was a red-haired man; he was also an earthly
man in his desires, and to satisfy an earthly gratification, he
sold his birthright, and a spiritual heritage went for a mess
of red pottage. To summarize, red or scarlet typifies the
fact that Jesus was human and that He was the Son of Man.
Here is a great contrast then:

Blue   . . . Divinity   . . . Jesus, the Son of God.
Scarlet . . . Humanity . . . Jesus, the Son of Man.

And now, between the two, comes a new color, blending
them into each other with wonderful harmony. It is:

Purple. We all know how to secure this color in paint. It
is by mixing blue and red. If we take the divine and the

human in Christ and blend them, what have we? A Mediator. "There is one . . . mediator between God and men, the man Christ Jesus" (1 Tim. 2:5). We shall consider more of the mediatorial glory of Christ revealed in the purple in the author's book entitled *These are the Garments,* on the high priest's robes. For this reason we leave it here.

Fine Twined Linen becomes the background of the rest, and how could Christ be all that He was and accomplish all that He did unless He was holy, perfect, pure, spotless, faultless, like the fine flour of the meal offering! Here then we see Christ as the sinless One.

With Cherubim. Cherubim speak to us of protection. We see them at the gate of the Garden of Eden keeping the way of the Tree of Life, and on the mercy seat guarding, as it were, the sprinkled blood. In the curtains they become part of the ornamentation of the ceiling of the tabernacle. The priest looking up would be reminded that God was looking down. So thought the psalmist when he said, "The eye of the Lord is upon them that fear him . . ." (Ps. 33:18).

Ten Curtains. These are another point of interest. There were ten curtains each twenty-eight cubits by four cubits. They were sewn together in two sets of five and then united by fifty golden taches in one hundred blue loops, making the total dimensions twenty-eight cubits by forty cubits. Ten is an accepted typical number for division. A few instances revealing this fact are — ten commandments, divided into two sections, one showing our duty toward God and the other our duty toward man; they were thus written on two tables of stone. Ten virgins were divided in their outlook — five were wise, five were foolish. Ten fingers are divided on two hands. Ten toes are divided on two feet. And here are ten curtains divided into two fives. How does this apply to Christ? There are two aspects of truth here.

1. Christ is a divider. Matthew 10:34b, 35, says: "I came not to send peace, but a sword. For I am come to set a man at variance against his father. . . ." But the Christ who divides is the Christ who unites with the taches of His

love. He divides us from worldly associates and unites us to Himself. He divides us from the old life, and links us with a new life which is with Christ in God.

2. Christ came to divide the camp of the Enemy, calling out a people for Himself and linking them onto God.

Fifty Golden Taches. In the goats' hair curtains you will observe that the taches are of brass, and that they link together the hundred loops, but in these linen curtains the taches are golden and the loops take hold of each other themselves. Here then is a progression such as can be noted everywhere in the tabernacle. The metals increase in value as we approach the center, brass to gold. The security also becomes stronger. In the first the taches hold the loops, in the second the loops hold each other and the taches become a double security.

When the curtains are in their place, the fifty taches lie immediately above the golden fillet which holds the veil, and divides the holy of holies from the holy place. Fifty again is the number of Pentecost. "And ye shall count unto you from the morrow after the sabbath, from the day that ye brought the sheaf of the wave-offering; seven sabbaths shall be complete: Even unto the morrow after the seventh sabbath shall ye number fifty days . . . (Lev. 23:15, 16). "And when the day of Pentecost was fully come . . . (Acts 2:1). This was fifty days after the resurrection. What happened then? The Holy Ghost descended and rested upon each of the disciples who were all filled with the power of the Holy Spirit. So the early disciples entered the dispensation of the Holy Ghost and of the Church. They surely could sing:

> "I have passed the riven veil where the glories never
> fail.
> I am living in the presence of the King."

The fifty taches prefigure all that Pentecost means. Pentecost in the Old Testament, Pentecost in the New Testament, surely implies Pentecost today.

8

THE COURT AND GATE

Exodus 27:9-19.   Exodus 38:9-20.

"And thou shalt make the court of the tabernacle: for the south side southward there shall be hangings for the court of fine twined linen of an hundred cubits long for one side: and the twenty pillars thereof and their twenty sockets shall be of brass; the hooks of the pillars and their fillets shall be of silver.   And likewise for the north side in length there shall be hangings of an hundred cubits long, and his twenty pillars and their twenty sockets of brass; the hooks of the pillars and their fillets of silver.   And for the breadth of the court on the west side shall be hangings of fifty cubits: their pillars ten, and their sockets ten.   And the breadth of the court on the east side eastward shall be fifty cubits.   The hangings of one side of the gate shall be fifteen cubits: their pillars three, and their sockets three. . . . And for the gate of the court shall be an hanging of twenty cubits, of blue, and purple, and scarlet, and fine twined linen, wrought with needlework: and their pillars shall be four, and their sockets four.   All the pillars round about the court shall be filleted with silver; their hooks shall be of silver, and their sockets of brass.   The length of the court shall be an hundred cubits, and the breadth fifty every where, and the height five cubits of fine twined linen, and their sockets of brass.   All the vessels of the tabernacle in all the service thereof, and all the pins thereof, and all the pins of the court, shall be of brass" (Ex. 27:9-19).

The Court.   This was a perfect oblong, twice as long as its breadth, being 100 cubits in length and 50 cubits in breadth; in English measure about 175 ft. long and 87 ft. 6 in. wide, standing 8 ft. 9 in. high. Its construction was upon sixty pillars, possibly of shittim wood (we are not actually told), set into sixty brass sockets which were buried into the sand for a foundation. Each pillar had a chapiter, or capital, which was overlaid with silver, and also a silver hook on which the curtains hung. Standing at equal distances apart, there were twenty pillars on the south side, twenty on the north side and ten on both the east and the west sides. They were all united to each other by a silver connecting bar called a silver fillet. Each pillar was made secure by cords fastened to brass tent pegs, called pins. Upon these pillars hung 490 ft. of fine twined linen, to which was added 35 ft. of blue, purple, scarlet, and fine twined linen. This made an entire enclosure; the 35 ft. of colored fabric, being in the center of the east end of the court, became the gate of entrance. This gate hung from four of the pillars. What was its purpose? It had several.

1. *It was a barrier.* It prevented unlawful approach to the sacred building, thus preserving its sanctity.

2. *It was a protection.* It kept wild animals at a distance.

3. *It was a distinct line of demarcation.* It kept the camp outside and the tabernacle inside. A great lesson is to be learned here. God has called for a positive mark of separation between the church and the world. Man desires to break down the barrier and mix the world and the church, while at the same time he seeks to set up very high barriers of sectarianism and denominationalism; the difference being, God has put the barrier between the world and the church and called for a life of separation, but man has moved it and put it between himself and fellow believers, thus breaking the fellowship of saints.

4. *It was to create a way of approach.* Man cannot come as he thinks. There is one way; God has provided it; and only by that way shall we ever approach God. That way is fully revealed as we study the furniture.

While the holy place remained the place for priests only, and the holy of holies excluded all but the High Priest, yet within the court all may come who will, priest and layman alike, those of high and low degree, the young and old, the rich and the poor, the reason being that it was the place of sacrifice and all needed its efficacy for without the shedding of blood there was no remission.

Just a word as to the typology of the court. It was a wonderful exhibition of righteousness. How the white linen of that court must have stood out in contrast to all the hundreds of black tents pitched on every side of it. Surely a picture of Christ's righteousness in the midst of a perverse and crooked generation.

The court is a wonderful picture of the Word of God, for the Word reveals how sin has been judged and put underfoot (brass sockets). It holds up as its head (silver chapiters) the redemptive work of Christ and, at the same time, displays on every hand the righteousness of God. The theme of redemption, running through the whole Bible, is sometimes called "the scarlet thread of redemption," "the hall mark of safety." Here it is seen as the silver fillet of redemption, extending to the full measurements of the court. From whatever direction man seeks to approach God, the law of God demands holiness, and exhibits holiness. Man is not holy, and cannot meet its demands, and so the curtains say: "Not this way." Does that drive man away a hopeless, helpless creature? Not at all. Paul says: "The law was our schoolmaster to lead us unto Christ," and so the curtains lead the sinner round until he comes to an entrance of blue, purple, and scarlet, on a background of righteousness. That entrance is Christ, the only One who satisfied the claims of the law. The One who said: "I am the way, the truth, and the life: no man cometh unto the Father, but by me", (John 14:6). In His righteousness I find my approach. What a picture! What a truth!! What a Saviour!!! But having been brought thus far, let us consider:

The Gate. It has much to teach us concerning the same

Great Person and the same great work to whom and to which all types point, and of which the tabernacle is a masterpiece of typology.

1. *It was an only gate*. Jesus said: "I am the way." How definite and decisive are the words of the Lord. There is but one way for salvation, that leaves man without question if he would but take heed. If the Lord had said: "I am *a* way," we might have considered other ways. If He had said, "Ye *may* be born again" we could have asked: "What else may we do." But no! He is definite — *The* way, *must* be born again. All who seek to enter in by other ways or by other means are thieves and robbers.

2. *It was a wide gate*. Thirty-five feet wide. Wide enough to receive "whosoever will," but with all its width it was still limited to a gate, and restricted to a way. It is of interest to know that it was the same size as the door of the tabernacle and the veil, although not the same shape. All three were a hundred square cubits. This gate had the breadth of universal access, for all may come although few do come. The other entrances had increased height that tells of exalted spiritual experience.

3. *It was an accessible gate*. How often we see gates and doors that are nearly always barred and bolted, opened only on special occasions and for special people. Then there are gates which need a porter to open them. There is yet another kind of gate, not easily opened. It is the gate of welcome into many communities of the Lord's people. A lengthy catechism may get it opened. How different are the things of God's providing. This gate is of a strong fabric yet it is easy to open, a child can push back a curtain, the aged can find access, the weak or the unlearned are not debarred for all know how to open so easy a gate. One thing must be emphasized here. There are so many pictures and diagrams that show this gate beautifully. looped back and fastened on either side, or else rolled up and made secure on the fillet above. This surely must be wrong. If it were thus folded why have a gate at all? Any wild animal

could roam in, any person could accidentally stroll through, and alas! alas! with such we meet constantly in everyday practical life. They are members of a church and "saved" quite by chance, somebody else did it for them, their circumstances of birth have brought them into a godly family. This is a condition of self-deception. No! the gate was closed, its beautiful colors exhibited, but it was not locked. It simply demanded the putting forth of the hand and the pushing back of the gate. Even so with our great salvation. May I appeal to you, my reader? Have you reached out the hand of faith and had personal contact with God, saying: "O, Lamb of God, I come." Conversion is not an accident, it is a real definite personal experience.

4. *It was an attractive gate.* Its wonderful blend of colors, standing out in beautiful contradistinction to the clear whiteness of the curtains, must attract the onlooker. Even so the glorious attributes of Christ stand out as a lovely relief from the holy demands of the law of God. The symbolism of these colors we have considered in the previous chapter, so a summary here will suffice:

Blue . . The Son of God satisfying the demands of God.

Purple . . The Kinsman-Redeemer, bringing God and man together.

Scarlet . . The Sno of Man meeting the needs of man.

Linen . . His holy character, making it possible for Him to open on our behalf a new and living way.

5. *It was a well-supported gate.* Four pillars upheld the fabric, so manifesting its full beauty. Mention has been made of the pillars of the court as representing the Word of God, holding forth God's righteous demands. May not these four pillars be designated as the representation of Matthew, Mark, Luke, and John, who show us much of the character, work, glory, and life of Christ. Matthew makes much of the purple as he portrays the Royal King. Mark sees more of the scarlet and tells us of a suffering servant.

Luke surely seveals the white linen of the perfect man from heaven. John ever remains the one to point to the blue and say: "Behold, the Lamb of God."

A final word — this gate will remain open as long as the Day of Grace remains. It is Christ, and He said: "By me if any man enter in, he shall be saved." The gate is the first step. It is the step of decision. Man today is undecided, but decision must come before acceptance, as repentance must come before forgiveness.

9

THE PILLAR OF CLOUD AND FIRE

Exodus 13:20-22.   Exodus 40:33-38.   Numbers 9:15-23.

"And he reared up the court round about the tabernacle and the altar, and set up the hanging of the court gate. So Moses finished the work. Then a cloud covered the tent of the congregation, and the glory of the Lord filled the tabernacle. And Moses was not able to enter into the tent of the congregation, because the cloud abode thereon, and the glory of the Lord filled the tabernacle. And when the cloud was taken up from over the tabernacle, the children of Israel went onward in all their journeys: but if the cloud were not taken up, then they journeyed not till the day that it was taken up. For the cloud of the Lord was upon the tabernacle by day, and fire was on it by night, in the sight of all the house of Israel, throughout all their journeys" (Ex. 40:33-38).

"And on the day that the tabernacle was reared up the cloud covered the tabernacle, namely, the tent of the testimony: and at even there was upon the tabernacle as it were the appearance of fire, until the morning. So it was alway: the cloud covered it by day, and the appearance of fire by night. And when the cloud was taken up from the tabernacle, then after that the children of Israel journeyed: and in the place where the cloud abode, there the children of Israel pitched their tents. At the commandment of the Lord the children of Israel journeyed, and at the commandment of the Lord they pitched: as long as the cloud abode upon the tabernacle they rested in their tents. And when the cloud tarried long upon the tabernacle many days, then the children of Israel kept the charge of the Lord, and journeyed not. And so it was, when the cloud was a few days upon the tabernacle; according to the commandment of the Lord they abode in their tents, and according to the commandment of the Lord they journeyed. And so it was, when the cloud abode from even unto the morning, and that the cloud was taken up in the morning, then they journeyed: whether it was by day or by night that the cloud was taken up, they journeyed. Or whether it were two days, or a month, or a year, that the cloud tarried upon the tabernacle, remaining thereon, the children of Israel abode in their tents, and journeyed not: but when it was taken up, they journeyed. At the commandment of the Lord they rested in the tents, and at the commandment of the Lord they journeyed: they kept the charge of the Lord, at the commandment of the Lord by the hand of Moses" (Num. 9:15-23).

We have made mention in a previous chapter of the sheik's spear and his use of it for command, observing that the pillar of cloud served similarly in the movements of the tabernacle and the camp. We will now glean some lessons from this "pillar of cloud by day and pillar of fire by night."

The origin of the pillar remains a mystery for we have not been told how it came, only when it came. It is introduced to us in a very matter-of-fact way. "And they took their journey from Succoth, and encamped in Etham, in the edge of the wilderness. And the Lord went before them by day in a pillar of a cloud, to lead them the way; and by night in a pillar of fire, to give them light; to go by day and night: he took not away the pillar of the cloud by day, nor the pillar of fire by night, from before the people" (Ex. 13:20-22).

The Typology. This pillar of cloud is a wonderful type of the incarnation of the Lord Jesus Christ. God was in this pillar to lead His people. "God was in Christ, reconciling the world unto himself . . ." (2 Cor. 5:19). It was not just a hovering cloud but a pillar of cloud. A pillar stands as an emblem of strength and stability, like those of Solomon's Temple. Christ was the strong one who was in the midst of His people. Not only was it a pillar of cloud but it was also a pillar of fire in the hours of darkness. So then, this symbol of the Divine Presence could never be erased. The "strong east wind" that blew all night and parted the waters of the Red Sea (Ex. 14:21) never blew this cloud across the sky. It remained, contrary to nature, "a pillar." The darkness of the storm cloud made it to become bright, yet the brightness of the sun could not dim it. It ever stood out against its environment. No weather prophet could explain it, and no scientist could explain it away. What glorious truth! Is it not the same with our Divine Leader? The storm of opposition and persecution cannot hide His blessed face. The bright sunshine of success should not dim the glories of the Lord; and neither the skeptic, atheist, nor modernist with all their materialistic arguments or bitter attacks will alter the fact that the Lord is in the midst of His people leading them all the way. WHAT WAS THIS PILLAR OF CLOUD TO ISRAEL? It was:

1. *A symbol of the presence of God.* From the time the symbol was given at Etham on the borders of the Red Sea until the tabernacle was built at Sinai it appeared to have had no particular abiding place, for we read of it in various places as in Exodus 16:10, it was toward the wilderness: "And it came to pass, as Aaron spake unto the whole congregation of the children of Israel, that they looked toward the wilderness, and behold, the glory of the Lord appeared in the cloud." In Exodus 33, the cloud appeared at the door of the tabernacle with Moses. "And Moses took the tabernacle, and pitched it without the camp, afar off from the camp, and called it the Tabernacle of the congregation. And it came to pass, that every one which sought the Lord went out unto the tabernacle of the congregation, which was without the camp. And it came to pass, when Moses went out unto the tabernacle, that all the people rose up, and stood every man at his tent door: and looked after Moses, until he was gone into the tabernacle. And it came to pass, as Moses entered into the tabernacle, the cloudy pillar

descended, and stood at the door of the tabernacle, and the Lord talked with Moses. And all the people saw the cloudy pillar stand at the tabernacle door: and all the people rose up and worshipped, every man in his tent door" (vers. 7-10).

It is quite evident that the tabernacle here referred to was not the tabernacle of the Lord which we are considering because, firstly, it was never outside the camp but always in the midst and, secondly, it was not Moses who entered into *the* tabernacle but Aaron. Thirdly, the tabernacle was not yet built. It was in all probability the tent or tabernacle of the elders that which existed prior to the tabernacle of the Lord. When the cloud descended upon this former tent it meant that God had come down to talk with Moses.

When the tabernacle was built and the glory of the Lord filled the place, then the pillar removed and took up its permanent abode over the Ark of the Covenant and the Shekinah glory. The pillar of cloud and fire then became the outward evidence to man of the inner glory of the Lord's presence.

2. *Their guide.* When it moved they moved, when it rested they rested. It mattered not whether it was for a day or a week, a month or even a year. This is stated in Numbers 9:15-21, quoted at the beginning of this chapter.

We learn from Israel's history that they ofttimes had to move at a moment's notice. Sometimes it was in the day and sometimes in the night. Let us look at the first move for an illustration. They were on the edge of the wilderness. Instead of moving straight forward, a map of their travels shows that the pillar led them down southward and they found themselves in a place with mountains on either side of them and the Red Sea stretching itself right across their path so that there was no way out. This caused Pharaoh to say: "They are entangled in the land, they are on easy prey." It would appear that God was driving the children of Israel to a complete destruction, instead of which He was actually leading Pharaoh and the Egyptians to their doom, for at the critical moment the pillar changed its position. How often the Christian has had such tests, but He is faithful, He faileth not.

On another occasion they were enduring the bitter experience of Marah but God led them on to Elim. There they enjoyed the shade of the seventy palm trees and the refreshment of the twelve wells. That was a pleasant change, they would stay awhile at Elim; but no! On they were led right into the heart of the wilderness, with no food, but really it was for them to learn how God could provide when they could not. Indeed it is true that:

> "God moves in a mysterious way
> His wonders to perform
> He plants His footsteps in the sea
> And rides upon the storm.
>
> Deep in unfathomable mines
> Of never failing skill,
> He treasures up His bright designs
> And works His sovereign will."

3. *Their protection.* At the time when they appeared to have been led into a trap at the Red Sea, the pillar moved from before them as a vanguard to take up its position behind as a rearward; but, in so doing, it came between them and their enemies, being to the one a source of help and blessing and to the other a cause of defeat. How much is this like the Cross of Christ! The Cross certainly stands between the believer and the world. To the believer, the Cross is his salvation; to the rejector, it is his condemnation. In this position the pillar became light to God's people and thick darkness to His enemies. That brings us to our next point.

4. *Their source of light.* Have you ever thought that, apart from this pillar, this great caravan of people had no light. They were in the wilderness. We talk of the modern inventions of our day, and include floodlighting as one of

them, but here was the first floodlighting effect. The pillar
of fire stood at the Red Sea and floodlit the path that God
had made through the waters. This pillar was God and
"God is light," and "If we walk in the light, as he is in the
light, we have fellowship one with another . . ." (1 John
1:7).

5. *Their shelter.* It appears to have opened out over
the people like a great umbrella. The psalmist infers this for
he said: "He spread a cloud for a covering; and fire to give
light in the night" (Ps. 105:39). So the sun shall not
smite thee by day nor the moon by night. And yet again the
psalmist speaks: "He that dwelleth in the secret place of
the most High shall abide under the shadow of the Almighty"
(Ps. 91:1). Our shelter at all times is the blood of Christ.
Finally:

6. *It is to be restored.* "And the Lord will create upon
every dwelling place of mount Zion, and upon her assem-
blies, a cloud and smoke by day, and the shining of a flam-
ing fire by night: for upon all the glory shall be a defence.
And there shall be a tabernacle for a shadow in the daytime
from the heat, and for a place of refuge, and for a covert
from storm and from rain" (Isa. 4.5, 6).

This is a prophetic utterance!

10

THE BRAZEN ALTAR

Exodus 27:1-8.   Exodus 38:1-7.   Exodus 20:24-26.

"And thou shalt make an altar of shittim wood, five cubits long, and five cubits broad; the altar shall be foursquare: and the height thereof shall be three cubits.   And thou shalt make the horns of it upon the four corners thereof: his horns shall be of the same: and thou shalt overlay it with brass. And thou shalt make his pans to receive his ashes, and his shovels, and his basons, and his fleshhooks, and his firepans: all the vessels thereof thou shalt make of brass.   And thou shalt make for it a grate of network of brass; and upon the net shalt thou make four brasen rings in the four corners thereof.   And thou shalt put it under the compass of the altar beneath, that the net may be even to the midst of the altar.   And thou shalt make staves for the altar, staves of shittim wood, and overlay them with brass.   And the staves shall be put into the rings, and the staves shall be upon the two sides of the altar, to bear it.   Hollow with boards shalt thou make it: as it was shewed thee in the mount, so shall they make it" (Ex. 27:1-8).

We have now come in our studies to the furniture of the tabernacle, every piece of which is charged with meaning and stands to declare the plans and purposes of God.   Upon entering the gate of the court we are confronted with the first and largest piece of furniture, namely the brazen altar.   The critic would say that sacrifice savored of heathenism, but one needs to remember that the heathen half followed truth.

Sacrifice is God-ordained. It was an absolute essential to Jewish worship. God must have taught something in connection with sacrifice to our foreparents when He made them coats of skin. The offerings of Cain and Abel were a demonstration of a possessed knowledge of altar building in connection with worship. It is interesting to note that after the deluge Noah built an altar before he built a house — Genesis 8:18-20 — and that Abram built an altar before he pitched a tent — Genesis 12:7, 8. Even so we must ourselves visit the "altar" and see our "Sacrifice" dying for us ere we can step into any blessing of a Christian walk or know anything of the fellowship of a living Christ. A word as to its

Meaning. The Hebrew word here is *mizbeach,* meaning "slaughter place." That is why, as we have just seen, the altar plays such an important part. That is also why it stands in such a prominent position. The law declares that without the shedding of blood there is no remission. In the use of the altar we learn that it lifted up the sacrifice in smoke; at the same time it would lift the offerer up into fellowship with God; while later, when the Cross became the altar for the world's great sacrifice, it lifted Him up so that we gaze on it and sing:

> "Lifted up was He to die
> 'It is finished' was His cry,
> Now in heaven, exalted high,
> Hallelujah! What a Saviour!"

"And I, if I be lifted up from the earth, will draw all men unto me" (John 12:32). The altar had but one

Purpose. Upon it sacrifices were to be consumed, so meeting and satisfying the claims of God. As a Holy God, He has irrevocable claims which must be fully realized before He can show forth mercy — sin must be punished, either in person or substitute. The lamb, goat, bullock, etc., were Israel's substitutes and God accepted them by means of the altar. These great claims of God have since been met to the full in Christ at Calvary, when He became the Offering, the Altar, and the Priest. Many types, metaphors, names, etc., are used to give expression to the all-sufficiency of Christ, who has met man's tremendous need from every conceivable angle.

Upon entering the court our attention is naturally drawn to the

Position of the altar just within the gate, easily accessible, unavoidable, and unmistakeable to the truly penitent inquirer. The altar was not inside the tabernacle but inside the court. It stood at the gate of repentance. Repentance is not salvation, it is only sorrow for sin. When a sinner comes to the place where he realizes he is a sinner, he must not only be sorry for that sin but willing to turn his back on it. Then it is he sees standing before him the altar:

> "And there before him stands the Cross,
> Two arms outstretched to save,
> Like a watchman set to guard the way
> From that eternal grave."

Many people see in the altar the end of things. This is only partially true. It is the end of the old life. It is the "It is finished" of Christ's redeeming work; yet, on the other hand, it is only the beginning of an holy walk and Christian experience. The altar then is only the first step in a new walk.

Let us now turn our attention to the

Size. Five by five by three cubits. It was decidedly the largest piece of furniture. It has been said that all of the other furniture could be put within its compass. Whether that was literally so, or not, seeing that two pieces have no stated size, remains a question; but of one thing we are assured and that is that every future blessing and the spiritual applications of the other furniture are certainly within the fold of Calvary, and all is ours because Christ's death has

made them so. Five cubits foursquare! Five is the number
of Grace. Hallelujah! It is all of grace, the unmerited
favor of God toward a sinful world. Such grace holds no
whims nor fancies, no partiality nor favoritism. It is foursquare, an emblem of solidity and equality. The three cubits
high might suggest to us that it was the third day when our
great Sacrifice was accepted by a satisfied Jehovah who de-
monstrated His approval by raising Christ from the dead.

We must not overlook the

Materials employed, although they have come under our
observation before. They were shittim wood and brass.
Shittim wood, or the acacia tree, grew with great profusion
on and around Sinai, where the tabernacle was built; thus
reminding us that the humanity of Christ, of which wood is
the symbol, was an ordinary humanity, not a specially prepared body that was exempt from suffering. "Forasmuch
then as the children are partakers of flesh and blood, he also
himself likewise took part of the same; that through death
he might destroy him that had the power of death, that is,
the devil" (Heb. 2:14). This wood was strengthened by an
overlay of brass, or it was strengthened for endurance. Had
not Christ been strengthened by His Father He would never
have been able to endure. His mental and physical weak-
ness were seen in such places as Gethsemane, when He sweat
as it were drops of blood. Again when He said: "I thirst,"
and "My God, My God, why hast thou forsaken me?"

Brass, as we know, is an alloy. It was unknown in early
days. Copper is the pure metal, and all historians, commentators, archaeologists, and others will support the fact
that brass refers to copper. Some people have criticized the
fact of wood overlaid with metal, suggesting that the heated
metal must burn the wood. A few years ago, at a time when
this nation was seeking to conserve metal, a "discovery" was
made by the scientists. They claimed that a door made of
wood and overlaid with copper, the joints of which were
hammered so that they were hermetically sealed, was absolutely fireproof. The invention was passed to the London

County Council Fire Brigade who put it through their tests. It stood all, and was certified "fireproof." This was considered a "modern invention," but it certainly answers the query of the brazen altar, and not only so but it stands as another witness to the accuracy of the Bible, and also reveals that the Bible is ahead of science and not adverse to it.

Our attention is now drawn to the

Design, the outstanding feature of which is the grate. It is generally accepted that the brazen grate had its position about halfway down inside. This theory I wish to refute, firstly on the ground of the logic of the context, and secondly, on the demands of the law concerning the altars of Israel.

1. *The context.* Let us read it very carefully. "And thou shalt make for it a grate of network of brass; and upon the net shalt thou make four brasen rings in the four corners thereof. And thou shalt put it under the compass of the altar beneath, that the net may be even to the midst of the altar. And thou shalt make staves for the altar, staves of shittim wood, and overlay them with brass. And the staves shall be put into the rings, and the staves shall be upon the two sides of the altar, to bear it. Hollow with boards shalt thou make it: as it was shewed thee in the mount, so shall they make it" (Ex. 27:4-7). The Hebrew word for grate is *mikbar,* meaning "twisted" or "plaited," and is only used here. It does not mean a sieve as some suggest. It was put *under* the compass. The word compass means "surrounding band" or that which encircles the outside. It is suggested that this band was a shelf on which to keep the mentioned utensils. That is immaterial except to suggest again that it surrounded the outside evidently halfway up — "in the midst" — that is, a cubit and a half from the top, and a cubit and a half from the botom. To put the grate under this compass must mean to put it outside. Again, four rings are to be put in the four corners, or extremities (original) of the grate and through these rings the staves, which were on the two sides of the altar, were to pass. This could not be done if the grate were inside. Furthermore,

the reference says "Hollow with boards shalt thou make it."
To be hollow it must be void of anything inside. This again
places the grate outside. On what then was the offering
made? This brings us to our next point.

2. *What the law demanded.* We are told in Exodus
20:24-26, "An altar of earth thou shalt make unto me, and
shalt sacrifice thereon thy burnt-offerings, and thy peace-
offerings, thy sheep, and thine oxen: in all places where I
record my name I will come unto thee, and I will bless thee.
And if thou wilt make me an altar of stone, thou shalt not
build it of hewn stone: for if thou lift up thy tool upon it,
thou hast polluted it. Neither shalt thou go up by steps
unto mine altar, that thy nakedness be not discovered thereon." This scripture would make it quite unlawful to offer
a sacrifice upon a grate because it would have been tooled.
It also suggests that the brazen altar was a case which would
be filled inside with earth or unhewn stone, whenever the
tabernacle was pitched. All this evidence puts the grate on
the outside of the altar, hanging beneath the compass. The
question is naturally asked — "Why was it there?" We are
informed that the altar possessed four horns and to these the
sacrificial animals were tied. There is a natural revulsion to
the smell of blood and death, and a resistance on the part of
the animal would take place, the mode of resistance being
to kick. This grate of brass surrounding the lower portion
of the altar would therefore protect the altar from damage.
Cannot we see the application? Bring the critic, the modernist, the atheist to the altar of Calvary, speak to him of
sacrifice and the shedding of blood, endeavor to tie him to
the truth of God's Word, and he will immediately kick
against the blood, denying its efficacy; but, blessed be God,
Calvary is surrounded by the Holy Ghost. Let them kick
as they will, they can do no harm. On the other hand, the
believer is called to yield himself a willing sacrifice, not a
resisting one. So much for the altar except a further word on
The Horns. These were peculiar only to Israelitish altars.
They were four in number, one in each corner. As symbols

of power and authority they pointed to the four corners of the earth. The horn of salvation, provided through the sacrifice of Calvary, points to every corner of the earth, saving to the uttermost, for:

> "Red and yellow, brown and white,
> All are precious in His sight.
> Jesus died for all the peoples of the world."

Sacrifices were bound to the horns of the altar of burnt offering because of their unwillingness. The psalmist refers to such an action: "Bind the sacrifice with cords, even unto the horns of the altar" (Ps. 118:27b).

Our Sacrifice was bound to the altar of the Cross by the cords of love. This is so beautifully expressed by A. M. Kelly:

> "Was it the nails, O Saviour, that bound Thee to the tree?
> Nay! 'Twas Thine everlasting Love, Thy love for me, for me.")

Then in turn you must "present your bodies a living sacrifice, holy, acceptable unto God, which is your reasonable service."

One or two brief reflections upon the appurtenances and the ritual. In this connection the number five repeats itself, in five utensils, five animals, and five offerings, standing out as further evidence of the grace which abounds at the altar. The five utensils were:

The Pans. These were used for the ashes, which are to be referred to again in a moment.

The Shovels. Their use was for picking up the ashes, and for tending or feeding the fire.

The Basons. They held the blood of the sacrifice which was sometimes carried inside, and sometimes poured out at the foot of the altar.

The Fleshhooks. These were for the arranging of the sacrifice in order upon the wood.

The Firepans (actually the "censers") were used for carrying the fire of the altar. With such censers Nadab and Abihu offered strange fire before the Lord and died (Lev. 10:1, 2). When the plague broke out because of the rebellion of Korah, Dathan and Abiram "Moses said unto Aaron, Take a censer [firepan], and put fire therein from off the altar, and put on incense, and go quickly unto the congregation, and make an atonement for them: for there is wrath gone out from the Lord; the plague is begun" (Num. 16:46).

The five animals mentioned were the lamb, bullock, goat, heifer, and turtle dove. Leviticus records the five offerings in connection with the altar of burnt offering. They were the burnt offering, the meal offering, the peace offering, the sin offering and the trespass offering; a subject we must enter into separately in future studies.

The concluding word is on the ritual of the ashes and the blood. Firstly,

The Ashes. But surely these were just thrown away! Not according to the law of the burnt offering, which demanded that "The priest shall put on his linen garment, and his linen breeches shall he put upon his flesh, and take up the ashes which the fire hath consumed with the burnt-offering on the altar, and he shall put them beside the altar. And he shall put off his garments, and put on other garments, and carry forth the ashes without the camp unto a clean place" (Lev. 6:10, 11). We shall not deal with the ceremony here, but with the ashes themselves. They were the last to be seen of the sacrifice; they were a proof that the sacrifice was taken and with solemn rites deposited in a clean place, afterwards to be used for the ceremonial cleansing of the unclean as recorded in Numbers 19. Even so, when we come to the world's great altar and the world's greatest offering — Calvary — we find that the evidence of the completeness of the work was the taking down of the body (the ashes) and placing it in a new tomb in which man had never lain (the clean place), from which He arose to cleanse the sinner.

To this the apostle referred when he said: "How much more shall the blood of Christ...purge your conscience from dead works to serve the living God" (Heb. 9:14). Lastly we consider

The Blood. It was never used, but poured out at the bottom of the altar. Man must not use blood or partake of it, because the life is in the blood, thus the blood poured out was a further evidence and a second witness to the fact that the life was poured out. When Christ gave His life, He gave His all. "Though he was rich, yet for your sakes he became poor, that ye through his poverty might be rich" (2 Cor. 8:9b). How poor He became! How rich we become!

11

THE BRAZEN LAVER

Exodus 30:17-21.   Exodus 38:8.   Exodus 40:7.

"And the Lord spake unto Moses, saying, Thou shalt also make a laver of brass, and his foot also of brass, to wash withal: and thou shalt put it between the tabernacle of the congregation and the altar, and thou shalt put water therein. For Aaron and his sons shall wash their hands and their feet thereat: When they go into the tabernacle of the congregation, they shall wash with water, that they die not; or when they come near to the altar to minister, to burn offering made by fire unto the Lord: so they shall wash their hands and their feet, that they die not: and it shall be a statute for ever to them, even to him and to his seed throughout their generations" (Ex. 30:17-21).

"And he made the laver of brass, and the foot of it of brass, of the lookingglasses of the women assembling, which assembled at the door of the tabernacle of the congregation" (Ex. 38:8).

What a little is recorded concerning this piece of furniture, and yet how important a matter it is! It would almost appear to be enshrouded in mystery. No statement is made concerning its shape or size, and when we read of the furniture being covered and conveyed the laver is never mentioned. In coming to such a subject we feel we are approaching the subject of sanctification, a matter so little understood and concerning which there are such variant doctrinal views. Let us consider first:

Its Origin. It was made from the looking-glasses of the women of Israel. It was their freewill offering, and we have every reason to believe that it was a sacrifice on their part even as it would be to many today. But then, what are gifts unless they really cost us something! One wonders sometimes why it was that they chose to give their mirrors rather than something else. We could easily say that a mirror is an essential to a neat and tidy person, and God never desires slackness; but then we have no reason to believe that they were mirrorless. Might it not be that they had caught a vision of themselves as God saw them, which had caused them to realize that the adornment of inward character was far more important than wasting time adorning the outward man which is ready to perish? It is interesting to notice how often we get a glimpse of New Testament truth in inspired actions of Old Testament people, for in this picture the mind will have traveled to 1 Timothy 2:9, 10, "In like manner also, that women adorn themselves in modest apparel, with shamefacedness and sobriety; not with broided hair, or gold, or pearls, or costly array; but (which becometh women professing godliness) with good works," and yet again 1 Peter 3:3, 4, "Whose adorning let it not be that outward adorning of plaiting the hair, and of wearing of gold, or of putting on of apparel; but let it be the hidden man of the heart, in that which is not corruptible, even the ornament of a meek and quiet spirit, which is in the sight of God of great price." There are but two ways of seeing ourselves, first, in our own mirrors where we have quite a good opinion of ourselves and yet a desire ever to improve our appearance, while the other is in the light and mirror of God's Word where we see ourselves as God sees us — that is, unclean — so that we say with Isaiah: "Woe is me! for I am undone..." (Isa. 6:5).

Its Form. It is often stated that nothing is said on this matter, but a little consideration will show that enough is said to enlighten the eyes of our understanding, and enough is not said to give us food for thought. We have with us

such sayings as "Actions speak louder than words" and
"Silence is golden." The silences of Scripture ofttimes
speak very clearly and loudly and are very precious.

"A laver and its foot" — that is the only description, but
there is possibly more in "its foot" than that which appears
in casual reading. It does not say a pedestal, but a foot,
and the Hebrew word means "base" or "station"; these could
be any shape. The writer is very strongly of the opinion
that it was in the form of a shallow bowl. A large upper
reservoir was the laver proper and a wide shallow bowl the
foot, the two possibly being connected by a pedestal. Now
as to the reason for such a design.

Eastern people do not wash in a bowl or basin, but always
in running water if at all possible. Ewers and basins are
commonly used for washing the hands and feet, the method
being to hold the hands or the feet over the basin and then
to pour the water from the ewer. Recent excavations at Ur
of the Chaldees have brought to light an early bath, very
shallow with an inlet and outlet for water. The bather
would lie flat and allow the water to flow through, thus
cleaning him. It has been pointed out that a fountain stands
in the court of one of the mosques at Jerusalem to which
the Moslems come for their daily ablutions. This is fitted
with taps from which the water runs into a lower basin and
thence drains away. To all this we may add an extract from
the pen of the late John Kitto in his notes in the *Pictorial
Bible:* "Our impression is that the laver, whatever were its
shape, stood upon another basin, more wide and shallow, as
a cup on a saucer; and that the latter received, from cocks
or spouts in the upper basin, the water which was allowed
to escape when the priests washed themselves with the water
which fell from the upper basin. If by the under basin we
understand the 'foot' of the text, the sense is clear. The
text does not say that the priests were to wash themselves
in the basin, but *at* it. *In* it they could not well wash their
hands and feet if the laver was of any height. The Rabbins
say the laver had several cocks, or 'nipples,' as they call

them, from which the water was let out as wanted. There were several such spouts, but the number is differently stated. How the priests washed their hands and feet at the laver seems uncertain. That they did not wash *in* either the laver or its basin seems clear, because then the water in which they washed would have been rendered impure by those who washed before or with them; and as we know that Orientals do not like to wash in a basin, after our manner, in which the water with which we commence washing is clearer than that with which we finish, but at a falling stream, where each successive affusion is of clean water, we incline to think that the priests either washed themselves with the stream as it fell from the spouts into the base, or else received in proper vessels so much water as they needed for the occasion. The Orientals, in their washings, make use of a vessel with a long spout, and wash at the stream which issues from thence, the waste water being received into a basin which is placed underneath. This seems to us to illustrate the idea of the laver with its base, as well as the ablutions of the priests. The laver had thus its upper basin, from which the stream fell, and the under basin for receiving the waste water; or it is quite compatible with the same idea and practice to suppose that, to prevent too great an expenditure of water, they received a quantity in separate vessels, using it as described, and the base receiving the water which in washing fell from their hands and feet. This explanation, although it seems to us probable, is, necessarily, little more than conjectural. The Jewish commentators say that any kind of water might be used for the laver; but that it was to be changed every day. They also state that ablution before entering the tabernacle was in no case dispensed with. A man might be perfectly clean, might be quite free from any ceremonial impurity, and might even have washed his hands and feet before he left home, but still he could by no means enter the tabercle without previously washing at the laver." The evidence is almost conclusive that thus was the form of the laver in the tabernacle of Israel.

Its Position. It was in the court where the priests ministered daily in sacrifices. It stood between the altar and the tabernacle. It was independent of the altar in position, but dependent on it for the blood that was sprinkled: "Moreover he [Moses] sprinkled with blood both the tabernacle, and all the vessels of the ministry. And almost all things are by the law purged with blood..." (Heb. 9:21, 22). It is important to note this relationship of the laver to the altar because of its doctrinal import, which we shall consider under our next heading

Its Type. After the aforesaid, maybe we shall be privileged to take up a new trend of thought from the customary one of the laver being a type of the Holy Spirit. This is rather premature. We shall meet truths concerning the Holy Spirit when we enter the tabernacle; the Spirit is for those who have clean hands and clean feet. John says: ". . . the Holy Ghost was not yet given; because that Jesus was not yet glorified" (John 7:39). What is it that stands out so pre-eminently, and yet so many have failed to see it just here? It is the Word of God. May we consider it from the points of view before us.

Firstly, the laver was made of looking-glasses. It revealed man to himself, so "by the *law* is the knowledge of sin" (Rom. 3:20b). The Word reveals our inability to live the Christian life in our own strength. The Word reveals much more. "For if any be a hearer of the word, and not a doer, he is like unto a man beholding his natural face in a glass: for he beholdeth himself, and goeth his way, and straightway forgetteth what manner of man he was. But whoso looketh into the perfect law of liberty, and continueth therein, he being not a forgetful hearer, but a doer of the work, this man shalt be blessed in his deed" (James 1:23-25).

Secondly, the laver also provided the necessary cleansing. Here lies possibly the greatest importance of its position, namely, beyond the altar. The altar was accessible to all, the laver only to the priests. The altar with its sacrifices was to deal with the subject of sin, but the laver was for those for whom atonement had been made. The Lord said to Peter, "He that is washed needeth not save to wash his feet, but is clean every whit..." (John 13:10). At the altar of Calvary the sinner was bathed, for "the blood of Jesus Christ his Son cleanseth us from *all* sin" (1 John 1:7b). At the laver the believer finds his daily cleansing from the defilements of life. He is thereby enabled to live a sanctified life.

The life of holiness is made possible by the Word of God, therefore may we stress the fact that the laver is a type of the Word of God, and not so much of the Holy Spirit who is inside the tabernacle working in the sanctified life. The best way to clinch this aspect of truth will be to quote the Word and so let it speak for itself:

"*Sanctify* them through thy truth: thy *word* is truth" (John 17:17).

"Wherewithal shall a young man *cleanse* his way? by taking heed thereto according to thy *word*" (Ps. 119:9).

"That he might *sanctify* and *cleanse* it with the washing of water by the *word*" (Eph. 5:26).

"Now ye are *clean* through the *word* which I have spoken unto you" (John 15:3).

You will, of course, observe that these references all apply to the believer. The unbeliever is always exhorted to find his cleansing in the blood of Christ.

Finally may we briefly note

The Instructions. "For Aaron and his sons shall wash their hands and their feet thereat: when they go into the tabernacle of the congregation, they shall wash with water, that they die not; or when they come near to the altar to minister, to burn offering made by fire unto the Lord: So they shall wash their hands and their feet, that they die not" (Ex. 30:19-21a). They who minister before the Lord must be clean. It was not a matter of opinion but a case of necessity. The priest had to wash every time he ministered, thus teaching us that one act can defile and make us unfit for service. Bearing in mind that we have taken the laver as a type of the Word of God, we have a great lesson to learn. It matters not whether we are going inside to minister to the Lord's people, or whether we are going to the Cross to point someone to the great sacrifice for sin, we must ourselves first go to the Word and see that we who bear the vessels of the Lord are clean. So many of the Lord's people have such a lack of knowledge and are so unacquainted with the Scriptures that they misquote, misinterpret, or adulterate them with their own ideas and fancies, and thus their ministry is anything but clean, and their life anything but "set apart" or sanctified; so that, while under grace, they do not die as was demanded by the law, yet their works are certainly dead. One needs to be well acquainted with both the Author and the Book, if anything in the way of a lasting and a God-glorifying work is to be accomplished.

> "I'm acquainted with the Author and I know God's Word
>   is true,
> In times of grief it brings relief, and tells me what to do.
>   Oh! I dearly love its pages, for I've found the Rock of
>   Ages,
>   I'm acquainted with the Author and I know 'tis true."

12

THE GOLDEN CANDLESTICK

Exodus 25:31-40; 37:17-24; 39:37.   Jeremiah 52:19.
Daniel 5:2-5.   Revelation 12:20.

"And thou shalt make a candlestick of pure gold: of beaten work shall the candlestick be made: his shaft, and his branches, his bowls, his knops, and his flowers, shall be the same.   And six branches shall come out of the sides of it; three branches of the candlestick out of the one side, and three branches of the candlestick out of the other side: Three bowls made like unto almonds, with a knop and a flower in one branch; and three bowls made like almonds in the other branch, with a knop and a flower: so in the six branches that come out of the candlestick.   And in the candlestick shall be four bowls made like unto almonds, with their knops and their flowers.   And there shall be a knop under two branches of the same, and a knop under two branches of the same, and a knop under two branches of the same, according to the six branches that proceed out of the candlestick.   Their knops and their branches shall be of the same: all of it shall be one beaten work of pure gold.   And thou shalt make the seven lamps thereof: and they shall light the lamps thereof, that they may give light over against it.   And the tongs thereof, and the snuffdishes thereof, shall be of pure gold.   Of a talent of pure gold shall he make it, with all these vessels.   And look that thou make them after their pattern, which was shewed thee in the mount" (Ex. 25:31-40).

We have now to examine the furniture of the Holy Place. Passing through the door, to which reference will be made later, we leave behind brass for gold, external for internal. The eye would naturally be drawn first toward the candlestick that stands to the left of the building. What a contrast! From a piece of furniture with practically no description to a candelabra with details that are profuse.

By way of introduction may it be said that it was not a candlestick after the modern use of that word; yet, at the same time, it is not an error or a misinterpretation of Scripture. The eastern folk had only a little clay lamp which burned olive oil. When in use they set it upon a tripod, or three-legged stand. This they called a candlestick, while the lamp they would ofttimes call a candle. Our western minds would call it a lampstand. This we must bear in mind when reading Matthew 5:15: "Neither do men light a candle, and put it under a bushel, but *on* a candlestick; and it giveth light unto all that are in the house." It is most obvious that the candlestick here is a lampstand because the lamps are referred to, also their trimming. This point we would stress as we open the chapter, because there is nothing in Scripture to warrant the use of candles in worship. The system practiced by some is absolutely erroneous and entirely foreign to the Word of God. Candles give light by the consumption of themselves, but the lamp gives its light by means of oil poured into it from time to time.

Shall we examine this piece of furniture more minutely? We learn that it was made of solid gold. Its weight was a talent, about 125 lb.; its face value as gold was about $30,000 at our present standard. This estimate does not include the cost of the labor put into it. While we shall consider all the detail given, in general it was a main shaft out of which emerged seven branches, three to the right, three to the left, and one directly out of the top. A base is not mentioned, possibly because it was part of the shaft.

Now let us meditate upon

Its Formation. "Of beaten work shall the candlestick be

made." The candlestick, the most beautiful, the most skill-
ful, the most ornamental, of all the pieces of furniture, was
not cast in a mold, neither was it made in sections and
assembled together, but it was beaten into its form and
beauty out of a solid block of gold; a task which we are
given to understand cannot be done today. Oh, the majesty
of God's plans foreshadowed in type! What a picture of the
unity of Christ with His Church! Could man do it today?
Could man do it at all? What could you and I see in a
nugget of gold? Just gold, that is all. What did Bezaleel
see in it? We can fully appreciate that Bezaleel and his
workmen were "anointed with the Spirit of God for all manner of cunning work." He must have had divine revelation
and guidance. Ask a man like Michaelangelo what he can
see in a block of marble and we can hear him say: "Beautiful! Lovely! ! I see there a group of angels, I see a lovely
figure, I see art!" But we say: "Where? We can only see
crudeness." Then he uses his mallet, his chisels, and his
master mind and he begins — chip, chip, chip, knocking a
piece off here, carving a piece out there, hard blows, light
taps, till after a long process we begin to see what he saw
all the time. That is how a statue comes into being — that
was how the candlestick made its appearance. That was
how the Church of God came to be. The Apostle Paul says:
"According as he hath chosen us in him before the foundation of the world..." (Eph. 1:4); while John speaks of:
". . . the Lamb slain from the foundation of the world"
(Rev. 13:8). Long before man saw the light of day, God
saw the Church as a beautiful body of believers "without
spot, or wrinkle, or any such thing." Long before man sinned, God in His foreknowledge planned His salvation in
Christ "For whom he did foreknow, he also did predestinate
to be conformed to the image of his Son" (Rom. 8:29).
Such a truth ought to make one shout for joy. We are not
linked on, not an afterthought, but one in Him and with
Him; eternally and essentially a part of Him by sovereign
grace. Surely this is eternal security! While God had thus

planned it in His purposes it was not seen until Pentecost, and not revealed in its fullness until Paul saw it and said: "This is a great mystery: but I speak concerning Christ and the church" (Eph. 5:32).

How came the Church into existence? By a beating process; for the Lamb was that block of gold. God Himself worked upon Him, for Isaiah says: "It pleased the Lord to bruise him" (53:10a). And what a bruising it was! In His birth He was unrecognized, unwanted; it was marred with poverty, no home, no bed. In His life He was despised, misjudged, misunderstood. He knew hunger and thirst, weariness of body and anguish of soul. He was robbed of reputation; His works were marred by unbelief. Then came Gethsemane and Calvary with the physical exhaustion, the lash, the nails, the sword, the crown of thorns, the mocking reed, the smiting, the spitting. Oh, the tragedy and the travesty! Yet through it all, His birth was a wonderful birth, His works were mighty works, His character was a holy character, His life was a perfect life, His body was a glorious body, His death was a triumphant death, His resurrection was a firstfruits resurrection, and it was all consummated by His ascending up on high there to make intercession for us, but not before He had promised to send another Comforter, the Holy Spirit; and with the descent of the Holy Spirit, there came into being that glorious body of believers called the Church which, through the ages, has ever been increasing and bearing its light and testimony, and will do until the day when He presents it a glorious body before His Father with exceeding joy.

This union of the believer with Christ is exhibited throughout Scripture. Eve was formed out of the side of Adam, and was "bone of his bone." Therefore the two shall be one. Christ said: "I am the vine, ye are the branches" (John 15:5a). "As the branch cannot bear fruit of itself, except it abide in the vine; no more can ye, except ye abide in me" (John 15:4b). Here we have the same simile, the main shaft being typical of Christ, and the branches of the believers.

Christ The Shaft.   The Hebrew word here translated "shaft" is *yarek* and means "thigh." Twenty times the word is translated "thigh," twice "loins," four times "side," and once "body." Genesis 46:26, Exodus 1:5, and Judges 8:30 show that *yarek* is connected with birth, "the souls that come out of the loins of Jacob," etc. What a matchless picture! Christ, the *yarek,* we proceeding from Him and yet of Him. "In him we live, and move, and have our being . . ." (Acts 17:28). A branch broken off from the shaft would be a useless thing. Being curved and having no base it would not stand and, therefore, could not hold a lamp. So are we apart from Christ. We are entirely dependent upon Him.

We The Branches.   It is not easy to ascertain the actual formation of the branches, but a quotation from *Young's Literal Translation of the Bible* may help.

> And thou hast made a candlestick of pure gold, of beaten work is the candlestick made; its base, and its branch, its calyxes, its knops and its flowers are the same; and six branches are coming out of its sides, three branches of the candlestick out of the one side, and three branches of the candlestick out of the second side (Ex. 25:31, 32).

What is to be noticed in this literal rendering at the moment is "its branch." In our Authorized Version it is "branches" in Exodus 25:31, but "branch" in Exodus 37:17. It should be singular in chapter 25. This makes clear the seven branches. The base, or shaft, and its branch, then six branches, three out of either side. Moreover, the "branch" has bowls, and knops and flowers, four of each, while the six branches have three bowls but only one knop and one flower each. Pictures and diagrams that have appeared in books, and other tabernacle illustrations, have never revealed this design because they are usually only artists' impressions. Do not think that we are too particular over the detail. In reality, we have not been particular enough, because the Lord God repeated several times to Moses: "See that thou make it according to the pattern." This emphasis is made because there is purpose in the pattern. The Lord would now say to us: "See that thou study and understand it according to the pattern." Gazing upon its form, lessons stand out clearly. The shaft, including the base, like the vine with its roots, is typical of Christ in His eternal and divine person from whom all believers emerge and upon whom the whole Church stands. Out of this shaft comes a branch called "His Branch." As we are informed that six branches come out of the sides, we must conclude that this branch came out of the top of the shaft as though a continuation, in which case the center shaft and branch must have stood pre-eminently high above the others. To see it thus is in perfect accord with Scripture because, in this branch, one can see the eternal Christ in His humanity made like unto His brethren and as one who is not ashamed to call us brethren, as we read in Hebrews 2. Yet another reference: "Therefore God, even thy God, hath anointed thee with the oil of gladness above thy fellows" (Heb. 1:9b). Six branches come from the sides, none from the front, because the believer must stand aside to give pre-eminence and glory to the eternal Christ. Six is the symbolical number of man, he who was created on the sixth day in the likeness of God, and who has come short of divine perfection. Here in the six branches is that man redeemed, and in the midst of them yet above them in the seventh branch is the Perfect Man, the Man Christ Jesus.

What an amount is said concerning

The Design. The pattern of the six branches differs from the seventh in detail but not in principle, because in all there are bowls, knops, and flowers.

The Knops will come under consideration first, because these are to be found in the shaft; there are three of them, one under each pair of branches. Great difference of opinion exists as to the actual appearance of the bowls, knops, and flowers. Therefore we can only weigh the evidence we have and draw a conclusion. Both Josephus and rabbinic writers say that the knop was a pomegranate, some suggesting it to be the bud and others the fruit, but, as the Vulgate and the Septuagint render it "ball" or "knob," we will harmonize all by accepting it as the fruit of the pomegranate which is a ball in shape, and is seen on much of the eastern ornamentation. In any case, the pomegranate is an emblem of peace, and is seen on the hem of the High Priest's garments, in the adornment of Solomon's Temple, and in the beautiful garden of love in the Song of Solomon. A round ball is a token of completeness or prefection. Thus, from the whole evidence, we can see "Peace, perfect peace." Three (the symbolical number of divinity) knops in the main shaft — God's eternal peace. Four (the symbolical number of earth) knops in the central branch — Christ's earthly peace. (1) At His birth, peace was announced, "Glory to God in the highest, and on earth peace . . . " (Luke 2:14). (2) In His ministry, "To guide our feet into the way of peace" (Luke 1:79b). (3) In His death, "Having made peace through the blood of his cross..." (Col. 1:20). (4) In His resurrection, "Now the God of peace, that brought again from the dead our Lord Jesus..." (Heb. 13:20). In each of the six branches there is one knop, thus teaching us that God's peace is our peace. The apostle says: "Now the Lord of peace himself give you peace always by all means..." (2 Thess. 3:16).

The Bowls. Referring back to the literal translation, the word "calyxes" is used, the original Hebrew word being translated "bowls" in the English version. The word is also translated "cup" in Genesis 44:2, 12, 16 and 17, and "pot" in Jeremiah 35:5. It occurs nowhere else: "Calyx" is a botanical term in use today and signifies a cup-shaped organ or cavity; the outer covering or leaflike envelope of a flower. The principal function of the calyx is to enclose and protect the other parts of the flower while in bud. The calyx frequently plays a part in connection with fruit dispersal. From this we conclude that calyxes of the almond

flower were included in the design of the candlestick. Our
hearts are gripped by the truth that, as the calyx protects
the bud of new life and also the seed of next year's life,
and in many cases is the progenitor of life, so Christ Himself
protects and. is the source of all life. "In him was life;
and the life was the light of men" (John 1:4). In Him
is the bud of human life and the seed of eternal life for
the whole world is represented in the *four* "bowls." As not
every seed in the botanical world germinates, so not every
possessor of human life believes unto eternal life. Three
calyxes were in each of the branches, reminding us that we
have received the life of the Father, and of the Son, and
of the Holy Ghost, and we can impart the blessings of that
life to others and so help to enlarge the Church of God
because "All things are of God, who hath reconciled us to
himself by Jesus Christ, and hath given to us the ministry
of reconciliation" (2 Cor. 5:18).

The Flowers. These are accepted to be lilies, and the lily
of Palestine is the wild anemone, such as Solomon in all
the glory of his array could not be likened unto. Lilies
with the pomegranates adorned the pillars of the temple,
and the same word "flower" *(tsists)* is used in connection
with the golden crown of the High Priest. Although a
fading flower, it is a picture of beauty. Four flowers on
"his branch" tell of the inconceivable and unsurpassable
beauty of the Man of Galilee. He showed the beauty of
holiness. He exhibited beauty of character in His life on
earth. While there were four flowers in the central branch,
there was only one in each of the other six. Did not the
psalmist pray: "Let the beauty of the Lord our God be
upon us"? The only beauty of which the Christian has to
boast is the beauty of Christian character. It is thus that
the world sees Jesus. Christlike character will always attract.
As these flowers were the crowning design of each branch,
into these flowers would be set the burning lamps of testimony. For what purpose were

The Lamps. Without the lamps the rest could be only

mere ornamentation. Beauty must be linked with usefulness. The purpose of the Church is to radiate light. It must be noticed that the light of the candlestick illuminated the tabernacle, it being in the Holy Place and not outside. We should be very concerned about our life in the Church — our witness before God and our fellow believer; because, if that is right, it must of necessity be right in the world outside. There are many professors in the Church who have a form of godliness but deny the power thereof. Of course, it was not the lamp that made the light, it only bore it. The light was resultant from the pure oil that was constantly being put within the lamp. Was not Pentecost the pouring in of the oil of the Holy Ghost making the Church, now formed by the sufferings and death of Christ which had just taken place, a bold, bright Church? This same Holy Spirit had been previously given to the lamp of the central branch when He was baptized of John in the River Jordan, and the Dove had descended upon Him. Jesus said, "I am the light of the world..." (John 8:12b). "Let your light so shine before men, that they may see your good works, and glorify your Father which is in heaven" (Matt. 5:16).

Reference has been made to the fact that it shone inside the tabernacle, not outside. To this end was it created. "And he lighted the lamps *before the Lord*..." (Ex. 40:25). The Church of Jesus Christ should ever remember that she lives before the Lord and she labors before the Lord. Singleness of eye and purity of motive must, therefore, be the incentive of all we do. Moses did not light the candlestick before the world, but the world knew the candlestick was alight. May we ever seek to live only for His glory, and the world will say: "These men have been with Jesus and learned of him." We are also informed that the candlestick stood opposite the Table of Shewbread (Ex. 26:35). Through the light of the Spirit manifested in the Church comes the knowledge, and the provision for fellowship as we feast with Him and on Him, the true Bread which came down from heaven.

The lampstand will send a beam of light onto the golden altar, and the veil before which the altar of incense stood. So it illuminated the place of intercession. Shall we not, in the Spirit, lift our hearts in prayer for the final rending of that veil, saying: "Even so, come Lord Jesus"?

Finally, "It gave light over against itself." If the Church shines before the Lord, it will unconsciously shine upon itself. Moses' face shone though he wist it not. He had been in the presence of God. Stephen looked steadfastly into heaven and his face was, as it were, the face of an angel.

Two small, but indispensable, things were attached to the candlestick. They were the

Tongs And Snuffdishes. The lamps would need to be trimmed; in fact, they were trimmed every morning and evening. During their hours of burning the wicks would burn low and the tongs would be needed to lift them up. Then too, soot will sometimes accumulate on the wick, causing the light to burn dimly. This soot was not caused by the oil, for it was pure, but by the consumption of the wick itself. So the tongs were needed to nip off the soot, and the snuffdishes to carry it away.

How often do things come into our lives that hinder our testimony, and cause the flame of devotion to burn low. Then the Lord comes with His tongs of reproof or chastisement to remove that hindrance; "For whom the Father loveth he chasteneth." We often blame the Enemy for attacks which are possibly the tongs of the Lord seeking to refine us that we may bear a better light. Let us allow the Lord to do that which He desires for our good, or He may say: "Repent, or I will remove thy candlestick from his place." The Lord may remove the lamp from the place of service, but we can rejoice in that He does not carry an extinguisher to put the light out.

13

THE TABLE OF SHEWBREAD

Exodus 25:23-30; 31:8; 37:10-16.   Leviticus 24:5-9.
Hebrews 9:2.

"Thou shalt make a table of shittim wood: two cubits
shall be the length thereof, and a cubit the breadth thereof,
and a cubit and a half the height thereof. And thou shalt
overlay it with pure gold, and make thereto a crown of gold
round about. And thou shalt make unto it a border of an
hand breadth round about, and thou shalt make a golden
crown to the border thereof round about. And thou shalt
make for it four rings of gold, and put the rings in the four
corners that are on the four feet thereof. Over against the
border shall the rings be for places of the staves to bear the
table. And thou shalt make the staves of shittim wood, and
overlay them with gold, that the table may be borne with
them. And thou shalt make the dishes thereof, and spoons
thereof, and covers thereof, and bowls thereof, to cover
withal: of pure gold shalt thou make them. And thou shalt
set upon the table shewbread before me alway" (Ex. 25:
23-30).

"And thou shalt take fine flour, and bake twelve cakes
thereof: two tenth deals shall be in one cake. And thou
shalt set them in two rows, six on a row, upon the pure
table before the Lord. And thou shalt put pure frankincense
upon each row, that it may be on the bread for a memorial,
even an offering made by fire unto the Lord. Every sabbath
he shall set it in order before the Lord continually, being
taken from the children of Israel by an everlasting covenant.
And it shall be Aaron's and his sons'; and they shall eat it

in the holy place: for it is most holy unto him of the offerings of the Lord made by fire by a perpetual statute" (Lev. 24: 5-9).

Opposite the candlestick, on the north side of the Holy Place, stood the table of shewbread with its twelve loaves. There is something charming and appealing about this piece of furniture. It speaks of fellowship, it is an emblem of friendship. When we desire to have fellowship with an acquaintance whom we may casually meet in town, we say: "Come and have a cup of coffee?" If we desire to know a friend a little more intimately, we wish to tell them things, and they to tell us things, it is customary to ask them home to a meal. How precious! The Lord of Glory desires fellowship with His redeemed ones! He desires more — that is that we should know Him better and He has, therefore, provided a table. David said: "Thou preparest a table before me in the presence of mine enemies." Here the table points to the one provided in the tabernacle for priests only. How plainly it speaks of the Lord's Table around which saints gather from week to week. We call it the Communion, or the Breaking of Bread. Do we know communion? The word means fellowship.

But let us come back to the table in the tabernacle.

Its Size was two by one by one and a half cubits. That is, the same height as the Ark of the Covenant, but half a cubit less in length and breadth, but when the handbreadth border with its crown is added, it is brought roughly to the same size. Measurements imply limitations. The table is large enough to receive all who are worthy to come, which is the whole priesthood, but small enough to exclude all who are not worthy. Judas having partaken of the first meal was exposed and took his leave before the institution of the Last Supper. No traitor should be at the Table of the Lord, nor yet any unbeliever. That is why the apostle said: "Let a man examine *himself,* and so let him eat of that bread, and drink of that cup. For he that eateth and drinketh unworthily, eateth and drinketh damnation to himself, not discerning the Lord's body" (1 Cor. 11:28, 29).

The Materials of this table correspond with those of the remaining furniture — shittim wood overlaid with gold. As shittim wood is that which tells of the humanity of Christ, while gold speaks of His divinity, so would we call to mind a twofold fellowship which Holy Writ shows to be ours. Firstly, the wood of His human life and His sojourning among men. What do we know of it? Paul says: "That I may know him, and the power of his resurrection, and the fellowship of his sufferings, being made conformable unto his death" (Phil. 3:10). Identification with His death means recognition in His glory, which is the gold of the table. Paul writing again says: ". . . that ye may be blameless in the day of our Lord Jesus Christ. God is faithful, by whom ye were called unto the fellowship of his Son Jesus Christ our Lord" (1 Cor. 1:8, 9). "If we suffer, we shall also reign with him. . ." (2 Tim. 2:12).

The table, as far as we have looked at it, was quite ordinary, but there were some peculiarities that made it extraordinary. It had a border, two crowns, rings and staves, all of which are very interesting to the child of God.

The Border, which was an handbreadth about four and a half inches, appears to be an addition to the table area. It is difficult to ascertain from the text as to whether it was on the same level as the table surface, or lower, as some suggest. The relief on the Arch of Titus, which is often referred to as a guide to this table and the candlestick, is no guide or help at all because that arch commemorates the destruction of the temple and the carrying away of its furniture, and we know that the style of some of the furniture in the temple was quite different from that of the tabernacle. One thing is certain about this border. It was extra to the table. Seeing that the lesser measurements are those of the table and that a table is not a table without legs, the border, as an addition, must have overhung the legs. The reason why we seek to emphasize this is because upon the table rested the twelve loaves while, possibly, the border with its crown became the place for the vessels of the table, namely, the dishes, spoons, covers, and bowls. The bread, therefore, typical of the Word of God, rested upon the sound foundation of the four legs, while the utensils had no foundation at all. Believer, do you not see that the only sure authority, the only certainty, the only food, is the Word of God? "Heaven and earth shall pass away, but my words shall not pass away" (Matt. 24:35). This Word becomes the food of the Christian. By it he is built up in his faith. The vessels we have noted found their place in the extended border. They were ordained of God and were used in connection with the table and the bread; but they were not food, and could not be eaten. Could not we liken these utensils to all manner of Bible helps — commentaries, concordances, studies, ministries, books (including this one)? While many of them are blessed of God, they are only to help us in our understanding of God's Word. We must not take these things as authoritative. They lack the foundation of divine inspiration and are not God-breathed. There is a great need today to call men back to The Book as the final authority.

The second peculiarity was:

The Crowns. There were two of them, one to the table and one to the border. Their purpose appears to be to keep things in their respective places. The first kept the bread to the table, the second prevented things from falling off the border. God has ever preserved His Word thus by the Holy Ghost. Some people would confuse things and mix the divine and the human elements, accepting man's word to be as authoritative as the Bible, but God holds the Book aloft as His. There are yet others who would push ministries and everything else of a spiritual nature to the background, but again the crown of God's Holy Spirit protects all who are, and all that is, sanctified by the Spirit. To change the type, the twice-crowned table of wood and gold would remind us of the twice-crowned Lord who provided for us the Bread of Life. In the wood of His humanity He

was crowned with thorns by wicked men. In the gold of
His divine life God has eternally crowned Him with glory
and honor.

The third feature of this table that distinguishes it from
other tables was that it had:

Rings And Staves, their purposes being, of course, to bear
the table. Tables usually have a permanent position. While
this table had its place and position, yet it was adapted to
its wilderness journeys. The people at this time were pilgrims. They traveled and the table traveled with them.
Here is a blessed thought — God has given to us spiritual
food, not in the form of a church or a ministry but in a
written word, in a book. We can carry it in our pocket,
or in a handbag. We can put it in our case when we travel,
by our bedside when we retire at night. I have read my
Bible on the top of mountains in solitude, on the bus amid
the crowds of London, in the subway rushing through the
bosom of the earth, in the hospital in the hour of sickness,
as well as in the church in the hour of worship. I have
found the opportunity for meditation at home in the morning,
at noon, at night, yea any time and anywhere — adaptability.

With regard to the

Vessels. Suffice it to say that, so far as evidence shows,
the *dishes or chargers* were used for the conveying of the
bread to the table. The *spoons* undoubtedly were used for
putting the incense on to the bread and possibly carrying
incense to the golden altar. Twelve spoons were given by
the princes according to Numbers 7, see verse 14, and every
sixth verse onward. The summary is in verse 86: "The
golden spoons were twelve, full of incense, weighing ten
shekels apiece, after the shekel of the sanctuary: all the
gold of the spoons was an hundred and twenty shekels."
Covers and bowls are the last two mentioned which, according to the Vulgate, Septuagint, Syriac, and most other
authorities, were "flagons" and "chalices." These vessels
were used in connection with the drink offering which always
accompanied the meal offering. Some of the drink offerings

were poured out at the brazen altar and some in the Holy Place. "And the drink-offering thereof shall be the fourth part of an hin for the one lamb: in the holy place shalt thou cause the strong wine to be poured unto the Lord for a drink-offering" (Num. 28:7). Those poured out in the Holy Place were not poured out at the golden altar, because "Ye shall offer no strange incense thereon, nor burnt-sacrifice, nor meat-offering; neither shall ye pour drink-offering thereon" (Ex. 30:9). The evidence then is that it was poured out before the table of shewbread where, we understand, the wine was with the bread.

So much for the table, but we must spend a little time on the most important thing, although reference has been made to it. It was not the brazen altar, but the sacrifice thereon that atoned. It was not the laver, but the water therein that cleansed. Neither was it the candlestick, but the light thereof that illuminated, nor the golden altar, but the incense that sanctified. Likewise, with the Ark of the Covenant, the blood-sprinkled mercy seat was the propitiation. Here at the table

The Shewbread was that upon which the priests fed. The full details concerning this bread are found in Leviticus 24:5-10. Reference has been made to the fact that the bread is a type of the Word of God, that is, Christ the "Written Word," but He is also seen as Christ the "Living Word." The loaves were to be made of fine flour. Nothing coarse or inferior would ever suffice in those things which pointed to the "Perfect One." The flour, a product of the earth, had not only to be ground in the mill but sieved, tested, and proved to be "fine" flour before it could be used for shewbread, or "presence-bread," or the "bread of faces" as it is sometimes called. This is a picture of the "Living Word." He not only passed through the mill of suffering, but He was tested and proved as "fine" and perfect in character. Here is the verdict:

Pilate said: "I find no fault in this man" (Luke 23:4).

Pilate's wife said: "Have thou nothing to do with that just

man" (Matt. 27:19).

Judas said: "I have sinned in that I have betrayed the innocent blood" (Matt. 27:4).

The malefactor said: "This man hath done nothing amiss" (Luke 23:41).

The centurion said: "Certainly this was a righteous man" (Luke 23:47).

God said: "My beloved Son, in whom I am well pleased" (Matt. 17:5).

He was indeed "Holy, harmless, undefiled, separate from sinners" (Heb. 7:26).

It matters not how fine the quality of the flour; by itself it cannot be eaten. It is, therefore, necessary to bake it. In the case of the unleavened shewbread it was baked in a fierce or quick oven. Was it not so with Christ? While His character was flawless and His life perfect, it could not meet the needs of failing man, or satisfy the demands of an Holy God — Christ, therefore, was pierced with holes all over, and then He passed through the fierce oven of Calvary and came out the Bread of Life, the Satisfier of those who trust Him.

There were twelve loaves perpetually laid on the table. They were eaten by the priests each week. Those priests, however many in number, were the representatives of God to the people and of the people to God. Therefore, as they feasted upon the bread representatively all twelve tribes feasted. God in Christ can and does provide for the whole Church.

Why did God tell them to put frankincense upon the loaves? We think of the spiritual application of purity, but as to actual and practical use we do not know. Did it sweeten the bread? We do know that Christ as the Bread of Life is not dry and uninteresting, but, rather, sweet to our taste, yea! sweeter than honey. Before the priests partook of the loaves, other loaves were put in their place; thus there was never any lack. None has ever come to the table of the Lord to find no food awaiting.

14

THE ALTAR OF INCENSE

Exodus 30:1-10; 37:25-29; 30:34-38.

"And thou shalt make an altar to burn incense upon: of shittim wood shalt thou make it. A cubit shall be the length thereof, and a cubit the breadth thereof; foursquare shall it be: and two cubits shall be the height thereof: the horns thereof shall be of the same. And thou shalt overlay it with pure gold, the top thereof and the sides thereof round about, and the horns thereof; and thou shalt make unto it a crown of gold round about. And two golden rings shalt thou make to it under the crown of it, by the two corners thereof, upon the two sides of it shalt thou make it; and they shall be for places for the staves to bear it withal. And thou shalt make the staves of shittim wood, and overlay them with gold. And thou shalt put it before the vail that is by the ark of the testimony, before the mercy seat that is over the testimony, where I will meet with thee. And Aaron shall burn thereon sweet incense every morning: when he dresseth the lamps, he shall burn incense upon it. And when Aaron lighteth the lamps at even, he shall burn incense upon it, a perpetual incense before the Lord throughout your generation. Ye shall offer no strange incense thereon, nor burnt-sacrifice, nor meat-offering; neither shall ye pour drink-offering thereon. And Aaron shall make an atonement upon the horns of it once in a year with the blood of the sin-offering of atonements: once in the year shall he make atonement upon it throughout your generations: it is most holy unto the Lord" (Ex. 30:1-10).

"And the Lord said unto Moses, Take unto thee sweet spices, stacte, and onycha, and galbanum; these sweet spices with pure frankincense: of each shall there be a like weight: And thou shalt make it a perfume, a confection after the art of the apothecary, tempered together pure and holy: And thou shalt beat some of it very small, and put of it before the testimony in the tabernacle of the congregation, where I will meet with thee: it shall be unto you most holy.   And as for the perfume which thou shalt make, ye shall not make to yourselves according to the composition thereof: it shall be unto thee holy for the Lord.   Whosoever shall make like unto that, to smell thereto, shall even be cut off from his people" (Ex. 30:34-38).

The altar of incense stood directly before the entrance to the tabernacle though further within than the other two pieces of furniture.   We are informed that its position was "before the veil."   It was only a small piece of furniture standing two cubits high and one cubit broad and long, or three feet six inches high and about twenty-one inches square.   It was just large enough to serve its purpose.

There does not appear to be anything significant in its measurements — we must not force the type just to make something out of it.   True it is higher than the table and the mercy seat, but it is in good proportion.   One noticeable thing is that it is definitely the smallest piece of furniture. That would not justify us in saying that it was less important than the rest, because that would be untrue.   Neither is it good reasoning to speak of its being higher in importance. There is a peculiar interweaving of truth that binds each piece within (or to) the other and makes them all indispensable, none being more important than the others because all are essential.   Might not the smallness of this representation of intercession remind one that it is not the length or the size of the prayer that prevails but its reality?   Did not the Lord say that we were not heard for our many words, for our vain repetitions?   Fervent, righteous prayer avails much. **The Materials** were again twofold, wood and gold.   Thus the *man Christ Jesus* makes intercession in *heaven* for the believing Church on *earth*.

A Crown kept the fire from falling to the ground. When the incense was brought by the priest, the fire was there to cause that incense to rise to God. Fire is one of the many descriptions used for the Holy Ghost. The Apostle Paul says: "The Spirit itself maketh intercession for us . . ." (Rom. 8:26b). The prayers of Christ never fail. Peter stumbled but, just before, the Lord had said to Peter: "Simon, Simon, behold, Satan hath desired to have you, that he may sift you as wheat: but I have prayed for thee..." (Luke 22:31, 32).

Horns were also to be found on this altar. Here they tell of the power of prayer, prayer that can reach to the four corners of the earth. Abram interceded for Sodom and prevailed as long as he prayed. Jacob wrestled all night at Penuel and became Israel. Ezekiel pleaded for Jerusalem. We need to lay hold of the horns of prevailing prayer.

Rings And Staves adapted the altar to wilderness experiences as they did the table of shewbread. Christ was ever in the midst of His people to hear their cry, and He still is. To the woman of Samaria He said: "Woman, believe me, the hour cometh, when ye shall neither in this mountain, nor yet at Jerusalem, worship the Father. But the hour cometh, and now is, when the true worshippers shall worship the Father in spirit and in truth: for the Father seeketh such to worship him" (John 4:21, 23). Intercession is limited neither to time nor place.

Its Purpose. The altar shows forth the greater work of Christ, who has already accomplished a great work. Having finished the work of redemption for the world, He went up on high to become the great Mediator between God and man, and the great Intercessor hearing our cry and pleading our cause. We, as the sons of the great High Priest, have received the same high calling in Christ Jesus.

Its position was in the direct line of approach to the mercy seat, therefore, before the Ark of the Covenant. The Ark was the dwelling place of God, He saying: "There will I meet with thee, and I will commune with thee from above the mercy seat, from between the two cherubims which are upon the ark of the testimony . . ." (Ex. 25:22a). The altar of incense holds the same position in heaven as it did on earth as can be seen in Revelation 8:3: "And another angel came and stood at the altar, having a golden censer; and there was given unto him much incense, that he should offer it with the prayers of all saints upon the golden altar which was before the throne." The only difference between the two is that once there hung a veil between, but now there is no veil, seeing it has been rent in twain and we have boldness to enter into His presence.

There appears to be special relationship between the three pieces of furniture in the Holy Place, created by the ministry of the priests between the one and the other. The principal link was between the candlestick and the altar. Verses 7 and 8 of Exodus 30 tell how the priest put incense on the golden altar at the time of the trimming of the lamps, both morning and evening. These were joint ministries. They always will be, prayer and testimony going together. It has been wisely said: "We shine best before men [the candlestick] when our hearts burn most before God [the altar]." This connection is readily seen throughout the Scriptures. Isaiah 6:5-9: "Then said I, Woe is me! for I am undone; because I am a man of unclean lips, and I dwell in the midst of a people of unclean lips: for mine eyes have seen the King, the Lord of hosts. Then flew one of the seraphims unto me, having a live coal in his hand, which he had taken with the tongs from off the altar; and he laid it upon my mouth, and said, Lo, this hath touched thy lips; and thine iniquity is taken away, and thy sin purged. Also I heard the voice of the Lord, saying, Whom shall I send, and who will go for us? Then said I, Here am I; send me. And He said, Go . . . ." Isaiah received a touch from the golden altar with his commission to "go" and minister. "I will put my spirit within you . . ." (the altar). "Then the heathen that are left round about you shall know . . ." (the candle-stick) Ezek. 36:27 and 36). "But ye shall receive power, after that the Holy Ghost is come upon you [the altar]: and ye shall be witnesses unto me both in Jesusalem, and in all Judæa and in Samaria, and unto the uttermost part of the earth [the candlestick]" Acts 1:8).

I have sometimes thought of this little piece of furniture standing before the veil as an electric plug such as we use to tap the electric power laid behind our walls. Behind the veil of the tabernacle was the Shekinah Glory of the presence of the Lord, and behind the veil of the sky are all the re-sources of the great triune Godhead. By putting in the plug of prayer with the hand of faith, we are able to tap those resources and find that "prayer changes things." Great things happen at the hour of prayer when incense is being offered. "And it came to pass at the time of the offering of the evening sacrifice, that Elijah the prophet came near, and said, Lord God of Abraham, Isaac, and of Israel, let it be known this day that thou art God in Israel....Then the fire of the Lord fell..." (1 Kings 18:36, 38). "Yea, whiles I was speaking in prayer, even the man Gabriel, whom I had seen in the vision at the beginning, being caused to fly swiftly, touched me about the time of the evening oblation" (Dan. 9:21). Then it was that Daniel received a revelation con-cerning the future of his people. "Now Peter and John went up together into the temple at the hour of prayer, being the *ninth hour*" (Acts 3:1). In their going they met and healed the lame man at the beautiful gate. "And Cornelius said, Four days ago I was fasting until this hour; and at the *ninth hour* I prayed in my house, and, behold, a man stood before me in bright clothing, and said, Cornelius, they prayer is heard..." (Acts 10:30, 31). The result was the gospel went to the Gentiles. "Now from the sixth hour there was darkness over all the land until the ninth hour. And about the *ninth hour* Jesus cried with a loud voice....Jesus, when he had cried again with a loud voice, yielded up the ghost. And, behold, the veil of the temple was rent in twain . . ." (Matt. 27:45-51).

The right use of the place of prayer brings much blessing, while the abuse of it brings a curse, "And Azariah the priest went in after him, and with him fourscore priests of the Lord, that were valiant men: And they withstood Uzziah the king, and said unto him, It appertaineth not unto thee, Uzziah, to burn incense unto the Lord, but to the priests the sons of Aaron, that are consecrated to burn incense: go out of the sanctuary; for thou hast trespassed; neither shall it be for thine honour from the Lord God. Then Uzziah was wroth, and had a censer in his hand to burn incense: and while he was wroth with the priests, the leprosy even rose up in his forehead before the priests in the house of the Lord, from beside the incense altar" (2 Chron. 26:17-19).

Before passing on to the incense, there is quite a contrast between the two altars which ought to be observed. The brazen altar was outside and the golden altar inside. The outside altar was made of wood and was strengthened with brass, the inside altar was likewise made of wood but it was beautified with gold. The first altar had no crown — Christ in His humiliation. The second had a crown — Christ in His exaltation. The brazen altar was the place of suffering and typifies Christ as Saviour. The golden altar was the place of triumph and typifies Christ as the Mediator. To the first came the sinner; the second was for the saint.

Beside contrast there is also similarity. Both altars were foursquare, which is a symmetrical sign of solidity and equality. At the one is seen Christ dying for the whole world, irrespective of color or race; at the other Christ is seen interceding for the whole Church of believers, irrespective of denomination or creed, providing they are "born again." Both have the rings and staves of non-isolation, and both have the symbols of universal strength — four horns.

The Incense. As was stated in the last chapter the value of the altar was in the incense. This was a mysterious compound carefully made with equal proportions of stacte, onycha, and galbanum with frankincense. Someone has beautifully typified this wonderful confection of equality with the great work of Christ as (1) merit of His life. (2) The merit of His death. (3) The merit of His resurrection, to which is added (4) the frankincense of His ascension. Which was the most important of these? None! for they are inseparable. His perfect life could not redeem, so His death was necesary. His death would not have been efficacious if His life had not been sinless, therefore, these are equal. Yet it needed His resurrection to show us that God was satisfied, and had accepted the work; while, if there had been no resurrection and Christ had remained in the grave, we would have had no intercessor, none to present our prayers faultless before God. The resurrection, therefore, was as important as the life and death. The consummation of His life work on earth was His ascension. We are not told what amount of frankincense was used, probably it was an equal amount.

"See that thou make nothing like unto it" was a very definite injunction given. "It is most holy unto the Lord." Could anything be made that would equal the compound of Christ's incarnate life? No! Then why did God give such a command? Because He knew that men would seek to make an imitation. There is but one "Mediator," but man has ordained his "priests" and established his "confessions." The Bible says: "Call no man your father upon the earth: for one is your Father, which is in heaven" (Matt. 23:9). Yet there is an order of men in certain sections of the church who are called "Father" and officiate as priests. Surely such is contrary to the Word of God and is an abomination in His sight. There is "one mediator between God and men, the man Christ Jesus" (1 Tim. 2:5b). "And having an high priest over the house of God; let us draw near with a true heart in full assurance of faith . . ." (Heb. 10:21, 22).

15

THE VEIL

Exodus 26:31-37.   Mark 15:38.   Hebrews 9 and 10.

"And thou shalt make a vail of blue, and purple, and scarlet, and fine twined linen of cunning work: with cherubims shall it be made: And thou shalt hang it upon four pillars of shittim wood overlaid with gold: their hooks shall be of gold, upon the four sockets of silver.   And thou shalt hang up the vail under the taches, that thou mayest bring in thither within the vail the ark of the testimony: and the vail shall divide unto you between the holy place and the most holy.   And thou shalt put the mercy seat upon the ark of the testimony in the most holy place.   And thou shalt set the table without the vail, and the candlestick over against the table on the side of the tabernacle toward the south: and thou shalt put the table on the north side.   And thou shalt make an hanging for the door of the tent, of blue, and purple, and scarlet, and fine twined linen, wrought with needlework.   And thou shalt make for the hanging five pillars of shittim wood, and overlay them with gold, and their hooks shall be of gold: and thou shalt cast five sockets of brass for them" (Ex. 26:31-37).

"And the veil of the temple was rent in twain from the top to the bottom" (Mark 15:38).

Six different veils are spoken of in the Scriptures.   They are:

1.   The Veil Of The Tabernacle.   Which is our study.
2.   The Veil Of The Temple.   "And he made the vail

of blue, and purple, and crimson, and fine linen, and wrought cherubims thereon" (2 Chron. 3:14). This was not the same veil as was in the tabernacle. Moses made the first, Solomon made the second. The veil of the tabernacle would have been useless in the massive temple, the measurements being extreme.

3.   The Veil Of Moses. "And till Moses had done speaking with them, he put a vail on his face. But when Moses went in before the Lord to speak with him, he took the vail off, until he came out. And he came out, and spake unto the children of Israel that which he was commanded. And the children of Israel saw the face of Moses, that the skin of Moses' face shone: and Moses put the vail upon his face again, until he went in to speak with him" (Ex. 34:33-35). The glorious character of the Godhead had secretly stamped itself upon Moses' face. The veil was necessary to conceal the glory from the mortal eyes of man.

4.   The Veil Of Christ's Flesh. "Having therefore, brethren, boldness to enter into the holiest by the blood of Jesus, by a new and living way, which he hath consecrated for us, through the veil, that is to say, his flesh" (Heb. 10:19, 20). The human frame that Christ took upon Himself was a veil which hid the inner glory of the divine life. Once in His life on the earth that glory burst through the veil, on the Mount of Transfiguration (Matt. 17:2).

5.   The Veil Of Unbelief. "And not as Moses, which put a vail over his face, that the children of Israel could not stedfastly look to the end of that which is abolished: but their minds were blinded: for until this day . . . when Moses is read, the vail is upon their heart. Nevertheless when it shall turn to the Lord, the vail shall be taken away" (2 Cor. 3:13-16). This means that, while they read the Law, they did not discern its principles.

6.   The Veil Of National Blindness. - "And he will destroy in this mountain the face of the covering cast over all people, and the vail that is spread over all nations. And it shall be said in that day, Lo, this is our God; we have waited for him, and he will save us: this is the Lord; we have waited for him, we will be glad and rejoice in his salvation" (Isa. 25:7, 9). The veil is over the scattered people of God, but, when it is removed, they will recognize Him whom they pierced and say: "Blessed is he that cometh in the name of the Lord." Then shall a nation be born in a day.

In each instance the veil is that which comes between and hides.

The veil of the tabernacle hung upon

Four Pillars made of shittim wood and overlaid with gold. The reason why there were four pillars to the veil in comparison with five to the door is obvious when we realize that the space was less, as the five pillars were undoubtedly on the front of the tabernacle, and the outer pillars butt in onto the edge of the first boards. While the five pillars of the door remind us of grace and their golden chapiters of sovereign grace that brought us access, the four pillars inside would tell us of the solidity of the work, as in the foursquare altars. The foundation of these pillars consisted of

Silver Sockets. Redemption is not only the ground upon which the believer stands but it is also the foundation and eternal purpose of Christ's Cross work.

The Golden Fillets above both the veil and the door remind us of the fact that the divine hand of God was ever upon His Son, upholding Him, and sustaining Him in all His earthly life.

The outstanding feature of the four pillars of the veil was that they lacked an architectural finish. Columns are usually finished with a capital. This you can see in all public buildings, in the Temple of Solomon, and in all the pillars of the tabernacle, with the exception of these four. No chapiter is mentioned at all. Is this an omission on the part of the writer? We think not, seeing that he was guided by divine inspiration. These pillars, upholding the veil that was to be rent, have a link with it, which has been expressed by the late Henry Soltau in the following words:

May not our thoughts be directed by this to the con-
templation of those scriptures which speak of the Lord
as cut off? Isaiah 53:8: "Who shall declare his
generation? for he was cut off out of the land of
the living." And Psalm 102:23, 24: "He shortened
my days. I said, O my God, take me not away in
the midst of my days!" And yet the very fact of this
seemingly abrupt termination of the life of the Lord
Jesus, in the days of His flesh, has made Him to be
unto us "wisdom, righteousness, sanctification, and
redemption": a fourfold perfection meeting our fourfold need; to which possibly the number of veil pillars
may allude.

The Veil. We learn from Hebrews 10:20, that the veil
refers to His flesh, His life upon earth. This was the "Word"
made flesh and dwelling among us, going about and doing
ceaseless good; but that was not the fullest manifestation of
the love of God. We are told that the way into the im-
mediate presence of God was not made manifest while the
veil remained unrent. So then, the veil is His life, and the
rending of the veil His death. His death, of course, was
the fullest revelation of the divine love.

The character of the incarnate Son of God is manifested in
the wonderful colors of the veil. We must refer the reader
back to the notes upon those colors in the curtains of the
tabernacle, in chapter 6. It was to be of

Cunning Work, or the work of a deviser, or an artificer.
We read that Bezaleel was anointed with the Spirit of God
for all manner of cunning work, and the work was undoubtedly cunning, not crude. Tradition says that the veil
was an handbreadth in thickness. It was a wonderful fabric
made according to a divine pattern. But no loom of earth
could have made the other veil "that is to say, His flesh."
But the same Spirit who anointed Bezaleel anointed also
the Virgin Mary for her special work of bringing into the
world that human frame which was to embody the incarnate
Godhead: "... The Holy Ghost shall come upon thee, and

the power of the Highest shall overshadow thee: therefore also that holy thing which shall be born of thee shall be called the Son of God" (Luke 1:35). "...She was found with child of the Holy Ghost" (Matt. 1:18). Born of a woman and yet called the Son of God (Blue). Called the Son of man (Red). Called Immanuel — God with us (Purple).

Upon this veil were skilfully wrought figures of cherubim, the emblems of guardianship. For while this veil was wonderfully wrought and beautifully attractive, yet its purpose was to keep out. It told man that he could not approach God. Christ in His ministry showed this. The apostle said in Hebrews 9:8 that as long as the first tabernacle was standing (dispensationally) the way into the Holiest was not made manifest. Even so, while Christ lived there was no redemption. But He died and, in so doing, not only opened a new and living way, but He brought the tabernacle dispensation to an end. And so we now see a

Veil Rent. "And, behold, the veil of the temple was rent in twain from the top to the bottom..." (Matt. 27:51). Simultaneously with the death of Christ on Calvary came this divine rending of the veil of the temple. So the way was opened — not to a mercy seat and an ark, for no ark existed in Herod's Temple. All trace of the ark had been lost hundreds of years earlier at the time when Solomon's Temple was destroyed. The death of Christ did not open the way to an ark, but to God Himself. Types are now fading away as realities shed forth their wonderful light. Christ dies to turn shadows into substance.

When referring to the veil, it includes both the veil of the tabernacle and the veil of the temple for, while they were materially different, they were doctrinally the same, just as I may move into a new house and change my furniture, but it is still home, because home is not the building or the furniture but the spirit, the love, the fellowship. This veil then was

1. Divinely Rent, from the top, beyond man's reach.

This is true of the death of Christ. "It pleased the Lord to bruise him." His own people rejected Him, Jews condemned Him, Romans crucified Him, yet He said: "I lay down my life of myself." With the rending of the veil came the closing of the old dispensation and the opening of a new. It was

2.   Rent In The Midst. The apostle said: "This thing was not done in a corner." Salvation is not something of which to be ashamed. Some people apologize for their faith. Paul said: "I am not ashamed of the gospel of Christ," and neither was God ashamed of it. It is a strait way, a direct approach. "I am the way...no man cometh unto the Father but by me." It was

3.   Rent Completely from top to bottom, not a thread was left. I believe the veil split and parted asunder exactly as the Mount of Olives will when Christ's feet touch it (Zech. 14:4).

Unfortunately, some people show us a veil with a rip in it, with many ragged threads of formality, ritual, law, doubt, "isms," etc., reaching from side to side, over which the sinner and the young Christian are caused to trip. But God has cleared the way, and left no obstacle at all.

16

THE ARK OF THE COVENANT

Exodus 25:10-22; 37:1-9.

"And they shall make an ark of shittim wood: two cubits and a half shall be the length thereof, and a cubit and a half the breadth thereof, and a cubit and a half the height thereof. And thou shalt overlay it with pure gold, within and without shalt thou overlay it, and shalt make upon it a crown of gold round about. And thou shalt cast four rings of gold for it, and put them in the four corners thereof; and two rings shall be in the one side of it, and two rings in the other side of it. And thou shalt make staves of shittim wood, and overlay them with gold. And thou shalt put the staves into the rings by the sides of the ark, that the ark may be borne with them. The staves shall be in the rings of the ark: they shall not be taken from it. And thou shalt put into the ark the testimony which I shall give thee. And thou shalt make a mercy seat of pure gold: two cubits and a half shall be the length thereof, and a cubit and a half the breadth thereof. And thou shalt make two cherubims of gold, of beaten work shalt thou make them, in the two ends of the mercy seat. And make one cherub on the one end, and the other cherub on the other end: even of the mercy seat shall ye make the cherubims on the two ends thereof. And the cherubims shall stretch forth their wings on high, covering the mercy seat with their wings, and their faces shall look one to another; toward the mercy seat shall the faces of the cherubims be. And thou shalt put the mercy seat above upon the ark; and in the ark thou shalt

put the testimony that I shall give thee.   And there I will
meet with thee, and I will commune with thee from above
the mercy seat, from between the two cherubims which are
upon the ark of the testimony, of all things which I will give
thee in commandment unto the children of Israel" (Ex. 25:
10-22).

With reverence and holy awe we step beyond the veil into
the Holiest of all and gaze upon the Ark of the Covenant,
a thing the Old Testament saints were never permitted to
do.   On the one day in the year when the High Priest did
enter, he dropped incense upon his burning censer, causing
a cloud of perfumed smoke to dim the vision.   As the veil
is now rent, we can come with holy boldness and learn all
that the ark once stood to teach us.

What Is An Ark?   The dictionary says: "A chest, or coffer,
for keeping safe and secret anything."   Bearing this in mind
there are three, if not four, arks mentioned in the Scriptures.

Noah's Ark.   "And God said unto Noah. . .Make thee an
ark of gopher wood; rooms shalt thou make in the ark, and
shalt pitch it within and without with pitch" (Gen. 6:13, 14).
This ark kept safe and secret eight righteous persons from
the judgment of God.

Moses' Ark.   "And when she could not longer hide him, she
took for him an ark of bulrushes, and daubed it with slime
and with pitch, and put the child therein; and she laid it
in the flags by the river's brink" (Ex. 2:3).   This ark
became the salvation of one baby from the wrath of a king.

God's Ark.   "And they shall make an ark of shittim wood:
two cubits and a half shall be the length thereof, and a cubit
and a half the breadth thereof, and a cubit and a half the
height thereof" (Ex. 25:10).   This chest hid the law of
an holy God, because man could not keep it.

Householder's Ark.   "Then said he unto them, Therefore
every scribe which is instructed unto the kingdom of heaven
is like unto a man that is an householder, which bringeth
forth out of his treasure [chest] things new and old" (Matt.
13:52).   It was the custom of eastern folk to keep a chest

in which they kept securely all their old heirlooms, and all their new valuables. When entertaining guests they would bring out their treasures and with pride show them to their friends. This chest was actually an ark although not so called here.

Position. The introduction to the whole subject is really arresting. "Let them make me a sanctuary...they shall make an ark." The very first detail given concerns this piece of furniture; the building itself comes later. We usually choose the furniture according to the building, but not so with the Lord. He commences where He always does, at the heart of things, working from within to without. The ark was normally the heart of the sanctuary; for a tabernacle without the ark would be like a body without a soul, or a Church without Christ. This is seen in Herod's Temple which had no true ark and was a system of religion and ritual which could do no more than crucify its Messiah.

A most detailed description is given of this piece of furniture and in every detail of it only Christ is to be seen. "They shall make an ark of

Shittim Wood." This wood is of a very hard, close-grained nature and one is often reminded of the lesson of durability, but as wood is a type of humanity there must be some deeper lesson to learn.

Shittim wood, we understand, comes from a tree which is a native of the district in which the children of Israel were then sojourning and where the tabernacle was to be made. If the Lord had said: "They shall make an ark of cedar wood," it might have involved a long journey to Lebanon. If it had been oak or gopher wood, they would have had to wait until they reached Palestine; for oaks do not grow in the desert. But, no! God chose to use the wood that was common to their environment and easily accessible. Oh, the wonder of it! When God chose to incarnate Himself for man by sending His only begotten Son, He did not send Him in the form of an angel or an archangel, nor yet with a mystical body belonging to some other realm. "But he

took upon himself the form of man and was made like unto
his brethren." Reverently we say it was just an ordinary
body, knowing the same temptations, the same physical
weaknesses and limitations, *yet* without sin. More of this
phase of truth can be seen in its

Size. It was two and a half cubits long, and one and a
half cubits high and wide. The ark then was restricted to
certain measurements. Even so Christ, in the flesh, was
confined to all our bodily limitations. His human strength
was limited; He knew tiredness and physical exhaustion.
His appetite was limited; He knew both hunger and thirst.
His natural abilities were limited to the same extent as ours,
that is to say, like ourselves He could only be in one place
at a time and do one thing at a time. It was not until after
He had laid down the natural, and had risen with a super-
natural body, that He was able to enter into a room with
doors barred and windows locked. When our mortal shall
have put on immortality we shall be the same. How suggestive then is shittim wood; but it was all

Overlaid With Gold, within and without. Gold, we have
already learned, is a type of divinity. What a wonderful
blending of the two natures — within the gold was wood
and within the wood was gold. The outward life of Christ
showed the gold of His divinity in His work, His words,
His whole demeanor. His inward thoughts and motives
were just as pure, just as holy. Some people's works are
good, but wrong motive robs them of blessing and reward;
some people mean well but act unwisely. How different
the Lord was! It has been said that the gold was beaten
onto the wood, and beaten so finely that the grain of the
wood showed through the gold. Whether that be so or not
is unrecorded in the sacred canon and its possibility is difficult to ascertain; but we do know that, amidst all the
demonstration of His divinity and power, the human nature
could always be seen. It was Divinity that said: "The
water that I shall give him shall be in him a well of water
springing up into everlasting life" (John 4:14b), and yet

He was sitting on the well, being wearied with His journey, when He spoke the life-giving words. Yet again, only Divinity could bid the waves obey His voice, but a moment or two before He bid them quell their fury His tiredness was acute enough to make the rigging of the boat a soft pillow for His weary head. Surely this is a wonderful blending of the divine and the human.

Round about this ark of dual material was a **Crown Of Gold,** solid gold. Man had crowned Him with thorns outside, but now He is inside and there God has eternally crowned Him with glory and honor. The next detail is: "Thou shalt cast **Four Rings Of Gold.**" This enabled the ark to be carried well-balanced. Being of solid gold these rings apply to the divine side of Christ's character. May we refer to them as four attributes of the divine character, as may also be seen in the four rings of the breastplate of judgment; the two rings on one side of the ark being attributes that are Godward — Justice and Holiness, while the two rings on the other side are attributes that are manward — Grace and Truth. Between the four rings is propitiation. Through these rings passed **Two Staves** made of shittim wood and overlaid with gold. Here the two elements are seen again, for Christ as man bore man to God, and as God bore God to man. On the ark was placed the **Mercy Seat.** A slab of solid gold two and a half by one and a half cubits. The mercy seat has no wood in it. Propitiation, of which the mercy seat is a type, belongs solely to God. The gold of the mercy seat has been valued at a figure exceeding $25,000. This would make it very precious, but upon it was sprinkled the blood of the atonement which made it priceless.

An extraordinary thing about this mercy seat was its name, because it was not a seat but a lid. The absence of a seat among the tabernacle furniture is an obvious thing, the reason of this, however, being that there was no need for one. The priestly work was never finished. The priest went on ministering until he was relieved by another, and so in relays the work continued. Only once do we ever read of a priest finishing His work and sitting down. He was the great High Priest. "And every priest *standeth* daily ministering and offering oftentimes the same sacrifices, which can never take away sins: but this man, after he had offered one sacrifice for sins for ever, *sat down* on the right hand of God" (Heb. 10:11, 12). The suggestion implied by the seat is, therefore, that of a finished work. In the administration of the tabernacle service there was no end. Christ alone could say: "It is finished" and when I come to Him I come to the end of my struggling, striving, and all kinds of self-efforts, and rest in Him and on Him. He is the Alpha (the brazen altar) and the Omega (the mercy seat) of our faith. We note that this was called more than a seat, it was a mercy seat. It was that which covered the law that had been deposited within the ark. Man could not keep it. That was proved when Moses came down from the Mount with the first two tables of stone and found the people worshiping the golden calf. So then, because man could not keep the law, God covered it with His mercy, and not through our accomplishments, have we found a resting place. We echo the thought of the psalmist when he said: "Surely goodness and mercy shall follow me all the days of my life: and I will dwell in the house of the Lord for ever" (Ps. 23:6).

Upon the mercy seat was the blood of propitiation sprinkled there every year on the Day of Atonement. The purpose of the mercy seat was to propitiate, as quoted in Romans 3:25: "Whom God hath set forth to be a propitiation [mercy seat] through faith in his blood, to declare his righteousness for the remission of sins that are past, through the forbearance of God." And yet again in 1 John 4:10: "Herein is love, not that we loved God, but that he loved us, and sent his Son to be the propitiation [mercy seat] for our sins."

We have yet to consider the

Cherubim. It is cherubim and not cherubims, as quoted in our authorized version. Cherubim is the plural of cherub. So we have two cherubim, "one cherub on the one end, and the other cherub on the other end: even of the mercy seat shall ye make the cherubims on the two ends thereof."

These cherubim were one with the mercy seat and of the same material. They are, therefore, inseparable from the propitiatory work of Christ. They have ofttimes been looked upon as representative of believers, in that we, as believers, are one with Christ, and also that we are to yield ourselves as willing sacrifices upon the altar. As against this, we point out that the mercy seat is not an altar; there is no sacrifice made upon it. The believer finds himself enjoying fellowship with Christ before the ark, because he has identified himself with Christ at the altar outside. Again, while it remains true that believers are one with Christ, the position held by these cherubim does not justify the claim here.

Cherubim are symbols of guardianship, as at the gate of the Garden of Eden. Here they are standing guarding the blood which is sprinkled on the mercy seat. The believer is never called upon to guard the blood, he ever stands in need of the blood to guard and to protect him. If the cherubim do not speak in some way of Christ, then the type has broken down on this one point because, not only have we seen Christ in each detail of this sacred chest, but we shall continue to see Him as we go on to study the contents of the ark.

They are Christ as the Word of God. The "Word" which was made flesh and dwelt among men, the two cherubim reminding us of the "Living Word" and the "Written Word," or Christ in all the Scriptures, Old Testament and New Testament. This is wonderfully borne out in the description given: "Their faces shall look one to another." This means agreement, for people turn their backs on those with whom they disagree. We cannot gainsay the fact that the Old and New Testament agree, the Old foretelling the New, and the New fulfilling the Old. The same applies to the "written" and the "living" Word.   God's Word is in harmony with Christ's life, and Christ came not to destroy the law but to fulfil it.

While these cherubim face each other, they are not looking at one another — that is, they are not occupied with each other, for "toward the mercy seat shall the faces of the cherubims be."   They were looking toward the blood.   The Old Testament in type and shadow, in doctrine and example, looks forward to Calvary and the shedding of blood, while the New Testament looks back to Calvary and tells us we are redeemed by the blood of Christ.   The wings are stretched out on high covering the mercy seat.   These are the pinions of protection.   Men would deny the power of the blood but the Word of God covers it, keeping it from all its assailants.

Between these cherubim and above the mercy seat was the **Shekinah Glory.**   The word *shekinah* does not occur in our Bible at all, it is a Hebrew word.   But here, in the Glory Cloud, did the Lord God dwell, and here it was that God met with Israel.   It is still the place where God meets man, for that place is between the pages of His Word and on the ground of shed blood.

17

THE TWO TABLES OF STONE

Exodus 19; 20:1-17.   Matthew 22:36-40.

"And God spake all these words, saying, I am the Lord thy God, which have brought thee out of the land of Egypt, out of the house of bondage.   Thou shalt have no other gods before me.   Thou shalt not make unto thee any graven image, or any likeness of any thing that is in heaven above, or that is in the earth beneath, or that is in the water under the earth.   Thou shalt not bow down thyself to them, nor serve them: for I the Lord thy God am a jealous God, visiting the iniquity of the fathers upon the children unto the third and fourth generation of them that hate me; and shewing mercy unto thousands of them that love me, and keep my commandments.   Thou shalt not take the name of the Lord thy God in vain; for the Lord will not hold him guiltless that taketh his name in vain.   Remember the sabbath day, to keep it holy.   Six days shalt thou labour, and do all thy work: but the seventh day is the sabbath of the Lord thy God: in it thou shalt not do any work, thou, nor thy son, nor thy daughter, thy manservant, nor thy maidservant, nor thy cattle, nor thy stranger that is within thy gates: for in six days the Lord made heaven and earth, the sea, and all that in them is, and rested the seventh day: wherefore the Lord blessed the sabbath day, and hallowed it.   Honour thy father and thy mother: that thy days may be long upon the land which the Lord thy God giveth thee.   Thou shalt not kill.   Thou shalt not commit adultery.   Thou shalt not steal.   Thou shalt not bear false witness against thy neighbour.   Thou shalt not covet thy neighbour's house, thou shalt not covet thy neighbour's wife, nor his manservant, nor his maidservant, nor his ox, nor his ass, nor any thing that is thy neighbour's" (Ex. 20:1-17).

"And thou shalt put into the ark the testimony that I shall give thee." That testimony was the moral law written on two tables of stone. The law of God, as given to Moses and as recorded in the Pentateuch, is threefold.

1. The Moral Law. Exodus 20:1-17. This consisted of the ten commandments which we are here to observe in particular. It governed the individual life of the children of Israel. This section of the law was indelibly engraved on two tables on stone and placed under the protection of the mercy seat.

2. The Civil Law. Exodus 21-33. Also Leviticus 11-15 and 17-20. This was that which controlled the national life of the children of Israel. It included such laws as those appertaining to murder, property, divorce, servants, injuries, etc. This, with the ceremonial law, was written in a book and kept beside the ark. "And it came to pass, when Moses had made an end of writing the words of this law in a book, until they were finished, that Moses commanded the Levites, which bare the ark of the covenant of the Lord, saying, Take this book of the law, and put it in the side of the ark of the covenant of the Lord your God, that it may be there for a witness against thee" (Deut. 31:24-26).

3. The Ceremonial Law. Exodus 25:1-40; Exodus 38. Also the greater part of Leviticus. This law ordered the religious life of the people. It embraced the subjects of the tabernacle, the priesthood, the offerings, and the feasts.

Looking at the subject still more broadly, law was a dispensation; it was the fifth of seven. They are respectively, the dispensations of (1) Innocence, (2) Conscience, (3) Human Government, (4) Promise, (5) Law, (6) Grace, (7) The Kingdom.

Coming back now to the moral law, this was given three times. The first time it was delivered orally. "And God answered him by a voice" (Ex. 19:19). "And God spake all these words, saying . . ." (Ex. 20:1). This statement is followed by the ten commandments. In verse 19 the people appealed to Moses, saying: "Speak thou with us, and we will hear: but let not God speak with us, lest we die." The Apostle Paul referring to the same occasion said: "And the sound of a trumpet, and the voice of words; which voice they that heard intreated that the word should not be spoken to them any more" (Heb. 12:19).

After this God called Moses to the mount again that he might receive the law in a written form. Exodus 24:12. "And the Lord said unto Moses, Come up to me into the mount, and be there: and I will give thee tables of stone, and a law, and commandments which I have written; that thou mayest teach them." It is to be noted that God provided the stones, as well as the writing. "And the tables were the work of God, and the writing was the writing of God, graven upon the tables," (Ex. 32:16). "And he gave unto Moses, when he had made an end of communing with him upon mount Sinai, two tables of testimony, tables of stone, written with the finger of God" (Ex. 31:18). As Moses descended from the mount with Joshua, he heard the noise of singing and beheld that the people below were worshiping a golden calf. Moses looked at the calf and then at the stones in his hands on which he read: "Thou shalt not make unto thee any graven image, or any likeness of any thing that is in heaven above, or that is in the earth beneath, or that is in the water under the earth. Thou shalt not bow down thyself to them..." (Ex. 20:4, 5). He listened and heard them say: "These be thy gods, O Israel, which brought thee up out of the land of Egypt." Then looking again at the tables he saw: "Thou shalt have no other gods before me." "Moses' anger waxed hot, and he cast the tables out of his hands, and brake them beneath the mount" (Ex. 32:19). The law was broken even while it was being made. We then find that God instructed Moses to procure two more stones. God cut the first but He did not make the second.

"And the Lord said unto Moses, Hew thee two tables of stone like unto the first: and I will write upon these tables the words that were in the first tables, which thou brakest. And he hewed two tables of stone like unto the first; and Moses rose up early in the morning, and went up unto Mount Sinai, as the Lord had commanded him, and took in his hand the two tables of stone" (Ex. 34:1, 4). "And he [Moses] was there with the Lord forty days and forty nights; he did neither eat bread, nor drink water. And he wrote upon the tables the words of the covenant, the ten commandments" (Ex. 34:28).

This law, which man could not keep, was deposited within the Ark of the Covenant and beneath the mercy seat, the type of the only One who kept the whole law. Moses reminding the children of Israel of their rebellion in Deuteronomy 10 says: "At that time the Lord said unto me, Hew thee two tables of stone like unto the first, and come up unto me into the mount, and make thee an ark of wood. And I will write on the tables the words that were in the first tables which thou brakest, and thou shalt put them in the ark. And I made an ark of shittim wood, and hewed two tables of stone like unto the first, and went up into the mount, having the two tables in mine hand. And he wrote on the tables, according to the first writing, the ten commandments, which the Lord spake unto you in the mount out of the midst of the fire in the day of the assembly: and the Lord gave them unto me. And I turned myself and came down from the mount, and put the tables in the ark which I had made; and there they be, as the Lord commanded me" (ver. 1-5).

A further point of interest in these tables is that they were written upon back and front. "And Moses turned, and went down from the mount, and the two tables of the testimony were in his hand: the tables were written on both their sides; on the one side and on the other were they written" (Ex. 32:15). Would not this often overlooked statement remind us that the law cannot be evaded? Man is full of excuses and might suggest to God that he did not know the law, maybe be came round the back side; but not so, wherever man is he must face up to the law; if not the law will face up with him. "Therefore thou art inexcusable, O man, whosoever thou art . . ." (Rom. 2:1). I cannot evade the law but I can escape it, but that only by being hidden in Christ who is willing to fulfil it on my behalf.

What was the object of writing the Decalogue on two tables of stone, and not one? It was not for reason of size because the stones were small enough for Moses to carry them up the mount and down the mount together. Was it not because the commandments were divided into two distinct sections? The possibility is there were four commandments on one stone, and the remaining six on the other stone. It is but a preconceived idea to put five on each stone. We are not told how they were divided, but we have more reason to believe they were four and six. The first four commandments reveal man's duty to God.

1. His Person. No other God before Me.
2. His Worship. No graven image or likeness to be made or worshiped.
3. His Name. Not to be taken in vain.
4. His Day. It must be kept holy.

The last six commandments show us man's duty to man.

5. Honor to parents.
6. Shall not kill another.
7. Shall not commit adultery with another.
8. Shall not steal from another.
9. Shall not tell lies against another.
10. Shall not covet the possessions of another.

The whole of the law appeared to be thus condensed and thus divided by the Lord Himself in answer to the lawyer who asked for the greatest commandment. "Jesus said unto him, Thou shalt love the Lord thy God with all thy heart, and with all thy soul, and with all thy mind. This is the first and great commandment [first stone]. And the second is like unto it, Thou shalt love thy neighbour as thyself [second stone]. On these two commandments hang *all* the law and the prophets" (Matt. 22:37-40).

The subject of the law is very vast, so we will endeavor to summarize it in a few quotations from the Scriptures:

1. It Reveals Sin (Rom. 3:20): "Therefore by the deeds of the law there shall no flesh be justified in his sight: for by the law is the knowledge of sin."

2. It Cannot Justify (Gal. 2:16): "Knowing that a man is not justified by the works of the law, but by the faith of Jesus Christ, even we have believed in Jesus Christ, that we might be justified by the faith of Christ, and not by the works of the law: for by the works of the law shall no flesh be justified."

3. It Leads To Christ (Gal. 3:24-25): "Wherefore the law was our schoolmaster to bring us unto Christ, that we might be justified by faith. But after that faith is come, we are no longer under a schoolmaster." This we can see working in every phase of life. The driving instructor is a tutor who brings me to the knowledge of driving. When the knowledge has come I need no longer a tutor but I go on driving with my newly acquired knowledge.

4. It Is Eternal (Luke 16:17): "And it is easier for heaven and earth to pass, than one tittle of the law to fail."

5. It Was Made Weak Through The Flesh (Rom. 8:3): "For what the law could not do, in that it was weak through the flesh, God sending his own Son in the likeness of sinful flesh, and for sin, condemned sin the flesh." It must not be understood here that the flesh first referred to is to the Adamic nature or the human nature. That did not weaken a perfect and eternal law. It was the flesh of the animals offered as substitutes for sin under the law. The offerings could atone for sin or temporarily cover sin, but they could not justify or redeem the sinner because an animal knows not temptation and does not possess sinful flesh. The law, therefore, came short of man's need, so God sent His Son in the likeness of *sinful flesh* to condemn sin in the flesh.

6. It was Fulfilled In Christ. (Matt. 5:17): "Think not that I am come to destroy the law, or the prophets: I am not come to destroy, but to fulfil." If we had an engagement and fail to keep it, we have broken our promise; but if we fulfil that engagement the promise then ceases to exist. This is exactly what has happened with the law. He did not break any of its precepts, but He did fulfil its demands. It demanded death — He met that demand and died. The law is, therefore, fulfilled and there is no death now to the person who believes it, for

7. Christ Is The End Of The Law, to believers only (Rom. 10:4): "For Christ is the end of the law for righteousness to every one that believeth." That means, therefore, that

8. We Are Not Under The Law (Rom. 6:14): "For sin shall not have dominion over you: for ye are not under the law, but under grace." This does not mean that the law does not exist. It means that I am insulated. An electric cable would injure and perhaps kill one who touched it, but if that person were to stand on a rubber mat and wear heavy rubber gloves he would be insulated, and while the power would remain, it would not harm him. So is it with the law and the man who has put on Christ Jesus as Lord. "If the Son therefore shall make you free, ye shall be free indeed" (John 8:36). We must not use our liberty as a cloak for maliciousness, for

9. We Are A Law To Ourselves (Rom. 2:14): "For when the Gentiles, which have not the law, do by nature the things contained in the law, these, having not the law, are a law unto themselves." In Christ there is neither Jew nor Gentile, but to the Christian there is a law of love and obedience. The old law said, "Do and live" — the law of grace says, "Live, and do."

18

THE GOLDEN POT OF MANNA

Exodus 16:11-31. Numbers 11:1-9. Psalm 78:24, 25.
John 6:31-38. Revelation 2:7.

"And the Lord spake unto Moses, saying, I have heard
the murmurings of the children of Israel: speak unto them,
saying, At even ye shall eat flesh, and in the morning ye
shall be filled with bread; and ye shall know that I am the
Lord your God. And it came to pass, that at even the
quails came up, and covered the camp: and in the morning
the dew lay round about the host. And when the dew that
lay was gone up, behold, upon the face of the wilderness
there lay a small round thing, as small as the hoar frost on
the ground. And when the children of Israel saw it, they
said one to another, It is manna: for they wist not what it
was. And Moses said unto them, This is the bread which
the Lord hath given you to eat. This is the thing which
the Lord hath commanded, Gather of it every man according to his eating, an omer for every man, according to the
number of your persons; take ye every man for them which
are in his tents. And the children of Israel did so, and
gathered, some more, some less. And when they did mete
it with an omer, he that gathered much had nothing over,
and he that gathered little had no lack; they gathered every
man according to his eating. And Moses said, Let no man
leave of it till the morning. Notwithstanding they hearkened
not unto Moses; but some of them left of it until the morning,
and it bred worms, and stank: and Moses was wroth with
them. And they gathered it every morning, every man

according to his eating: and when the sun waxed hot, it melted. And it came to pass, that on the sixth day they gathered twice as much bread, two omers for one man: and all the rulers of the congregation came and told Moses. And he said unto them, This is that which the Lord hath said, Tomorrow is the rest of the holy sabbath unto the Lord: bake that which ye will bake today, and seethe that ye will seethe; and that which remaineth over lay up for you to be kept until the morning. And they laid it up till the morning, as Moses bade: and it did not stink, neither was there any worm therein. And Moses said, Eat that today; for today is a sabbath unto the Lord: today ye shall not find it in the field. Six days ye shall gather it; but on the seventh day, which is the sabbath, in it there shall be none. And it came to pass, that there went out some of the people on the seventh day for to gather, and they found none. And the Lord said unto Moses, How long refuse ye to keep my commandments, and my laws? See, for that the Lord hath given you the sabbath, therefore he giveth you on the sixth day the bread of two days; abide ye every man in his place, let no man go out of his place on the seventh day. So the people rested on the seventh day. And the house of Israel called the name thereof Manna: and it was like coriander seed, white; and the taste of it was like wafers made with honey" (Ex. 16:11-31).

"And the manna was as coriander seed, and the colour thereof as the colour of bdellium. And the people went about, and gathered it, and ground it in mills, or beat it in a mortar, and baked it in pans, and made cakes of it: and the taste of it was as the taste of fresh oil. And when the dew fell upon the camp in the night, the manna fell upon it" (Num. 11:7-9).

When the children of Israel first saw the bread of God's providing they said: "It is manna." There are three interpretations to the word "manna." They are:

Hebrew	. . . . . .	"What is it?"
Chaldean	. . . . . .	"It is a portion."
English	. . . . .	"Bread."

The people were soon to learn what it really was. It was to be their food while they journeyed. Jesus said that He was the "Bread of Life" He also said: "I am the true bread which came down from heaven." The world still looks on, and of Christ and the Word of God they are saying: "What is it?" The true believer is he that can use the word in the Chaldean sense and say, concerning the Word of God: "It is a portion," and concerning Christ Himself, "He is a portion."

What kind of a portion was the manna to this army of pilgrims? It was a

Sufficient Portion. There was enough for all and no lack.

Suitable Portion. It suited every palate, young and old alike, also the weak and the strong. The Jews say, "It tasted to every man as he pleased."

Satisfying Portion. No man ever went hungry. "The young lions do lack, and suffer hunger; but they that seek the Lord shall not want any good thing."

Strengthening Portion. It made strong men of them. They were able to journey in a desert, to work, and to fight.

Sustaining Portion. On it they lived for forty years. It must have been very nutritious.

Sure Portion. It never failed.

Cannot all this be said of Christ Jesus our Lord? There is an all-sufficiency in Him. He suits all classes, all nationalities, all ages, yea, all men everywhere. He certainly satisfies those who trust Him. "All that I want is in Jesus, He satisfies, joy He supplies. Life would be worthless without Him, All things in Jesus I find." He also strengthens His followers for life and service. He will sustain us all through life's journey and will never fail. Joshua tells us that there was an overlap in the supply of manna. "And the manna ceased on the morrow after they had eaten of the old corn of the land" (Josh. 5:12). Christ is not only our supply in life but He will take us through until we get right into the heavenly land to feast upon "hidden manna."

What a wonderful description is given to us of so small

an object. This is because it is typical of Christ as the
Bread of Life, and the description shows forth His character,
as follows:

Description	Type
Small	Humility of Christ.
Round	Perfection of His Life.
White	Purity of His character.
Like Hoar Frost .	Crisp, energizing life He imparts.
Like Coriander Seed: . . .	
(a) Aromatic when crushed	Fragrance of the suffering Man of Calvary.
(b) A herb .	Health of mankind.
As fresh oil . .	Anointing of the Holy Spirit.
As honey . . .	Sweetness of the "Word of God."
As bdellium . . (White pearl.)	"The Pearl of Greatest Price."

This is a matchless picture of the Christ whom we serve.
Has not God promised to supply all our needs according
to His riches in glory by Christ Jesus! Well may we sing:

> "I've found the Pearl of Greatest price,
> My heart doth sing for joy;
> And sing I must, for Christ I have —
> Oh! what a Christ have I !
> Christ is my Meat, Christ is my Drink,
> My Medicine and my Health,
> My Portion, mine Inheritance,
> Yea, all my Boundless Wealth."

We will now consider
How It Came. (1) *Every morning.* In the manna we
see Christ as both the "Living Word" and the "Written
Word," but more particularly as the latter. As "a portion"

we see Him in both ways. In the description of the manna He is seen as the "Living Word." But now in the instructions we see Him as the "Written Word." The Lord would encourage us in a daily reading of His Word, and that at the beginning of the day.

(2) *Around the camp.* That is, it was within the reach of all. There is a community of people that put the church on earth in a superior place to the Bible. They would tell us that the church has received full and final authority. This would mean that some could never get a daily supply from God; sickness, business, distance, weather, and a score of other reasons preventing, but God has given us His Word in the form of a written oracle or a book. It is in the camp; it is always within reach.

(3) *With the dew.* "And when the dew fell upon the camp in the night, the manna fell upon it" (Num. 11:9). "And when the dew that lay was gone up, behold, upon the face of the wilderness there lay a small round thing, as small as the hoar frost on the ground" (Ex. 16:14). It would appear from these two scriptures that the dew was both underneath and on the top of the manna, thus enwrapping it and keeping it fresh and clean. It was the moving of the dew that revealed the manna. The dew is one of the symbols of the Holy Spirit. I may have the Word of God within my reach. I may read it and not profit thereby. Carnal and critical minds never do benefit from thus reading. It was when the dew lifted that the manna was revealed, and it is by the moving of the Spirit that divine revelation comes to us. For "When he, the Spirit of truth, is come, he will guide you into all truth..." (John 16:13).

God then gave a number of

Instructions to control the allocation of the divine provision.

(1) *The head of the house was to gather for all within.* "This is the thing which the Lord hath commanded, Gather of it every man according to his eating, an omer for every man, according to the number of your persons; take ye every man for them which are in his tents" (Ex. 16:16). "Ac-

cording to his eating" means according to the size of his
family. It is important to note that the Lord told the men
to gather for those inside his tent, namely, the women and
the children. In the East the women do much of the man-
ual and the menial work, grinding corn, drawing water,
etc., but now the man is instructed so to do. Not only is
it the duty and the privilege of the man, as the head of the
house, to collect and distribute spiritual food at the morning
reading and prayers of the family, but it is the duty of us
all to minister to those who cannot gather for themselves.
In this injunction comes a great call for family worship.

(2) *At the rate of an omer per head.* It was an equal
portion for all. It was as much for the maid as for the
mistress, and for the servant as the master; as much for the
women as for the men. It was equally as much for the
child and "for the stranger within thy gates."

(3) *One day's portion at a time (except the sixth day).*
God's gifts are always given as needed. The harvest of the
whole world has only an overlap of six weeks. We live by
faith. God has promised to meet our needs day by day
and He will not fail us. Because no manner of work was
to be done on the sabbath day, He made provision on the
sixth day for a double supply. God always will provide for
the man who honors Him by the keeping of the Lord's day,
the one in seven. We are now living in an age when the
Lord's day is being sadly neglected by the world, and slackly
used by the Church. Christians now travel on Sunday without any concern. They stay away from the house of God
to cook the dinner. They write and mail letters on a Sunday,
which could easily be done on Monday, but as a result they
are losing much of the joy of the Lord. God must and will
honor those who honor Him.

Looking at the matter more broadly, one may meet a
period in life when the source of outward supply is cut off
temporarily by uncontrollable circumstances. Then we shall
find that God has given us a source of inward supply that
has unconsciously come to us through the faithful gathering

of the past.

(4) *None were to have a surplus.* God never encouraged a storage which meant selfishness or lack of trust. Some people seem to find surplus. They will refer to certain parts of God's Word, or to some doctrines, principles or commands, as unnecessary. Something with which they can do without. The modernist appears to find a good deal of surplus in the Bible. God says there is nothing over; that every word is profitable, and is for our learning. But while there is no surplus, God is not mean, for

(5) *None were to lack anything* (ver. 18). God gives according to our ability. Believing that I shall lack nothing, I must use all. The writer remembers an occasion when, as a lad just beginning to speak in open-air meetings and in small ways, he received one day a blessing and a message from the Word of God. He was so pleased about it that he decided not to pass it on but to keep it for some special occasion when he might be asked to speak at a larger meeting, but when the "larger meeting" came he could not remember that message. He tried hard, but he had forgotten it. He had lost it. It had "bred worms and stank." He learned his lesson as a lad, and since then has always sought at all times to give the best.

(6) *The sun cleansed the earth after the morning gathering.* This surely tells us to make much of present opportunities or we may lose everything.

Methods Of Use. "...Bake that which ye will bake to day, and seethe that ye will seethe..." (Ex. 16:23). "And the people went about, and gathered it, and ground it in mills, or beat it in a mortar, and baked it in pans, and made cakes of it..." (Num. 11:8). From these two verses we see that a variety of methods were used in preparing the manna for consumption. It could be ground in the grindstones like corn, or it could be beaten in the mortar. It could be baked, or boiled, or made into cakes for the child. We may classify it in this way:

Baked	. . .	for the strong	. Strong Meat.
Seethed	. . .	for the weaker	. Bread.
Ground or Beaten	for the simple	.	
		or aged .	. Sincere milk.
Made into cakes	for the child	. Royal dainties.	

We may take the Word of God and study it as we will for profit; dispensationally or doctrinally for the strong in faith; book, text or character for the weaker in faith; or the parables, stories and miracles of Christ for the young in faith. We may take the Bible and grind it up, breaking it as small as we wish, as the botanist does with his analysis of the flower and the chemist with his chemistry. We shall profit by so doing, *but* we must not tear the Book up and pull it to pieces as the critic and the modernist do. Honest criticism is good and profitable; critical criticism is wrong and disastrous. This is seen in rather an extraordinary way in our lesson, for the manna would stand beating and grinding; yet, at the rising of the morning sun, it disappeared like the dew. Divine revelation and knowledge will always flee before the rays of modernistic and materialistic thought, leaving the thinkers starving and dissatisfied, not because it is afraid or cannot face the modernist, but because ". . . thou hast hid these things from the wise and prudent, and hast revealed them unto babes" (Matt. 11:25).

Final Application. Christ very ably showed Himself to be the great antitype of the manna in John 6. The Jews had ever given Moses the credit of supplying their forefathers with the manna in the wilderness. Alas! God is still ofttimes robbed of glory and praise of which He alone is worthy. So He reasons with the crowd, and says: "Verily, verily, I say unto you, Moses gave you not that bread from heaven; but my Father giveth you the true bread from heaven. For the bread of God is he which cometh down from heaven and giveth life unto the world. . . . I am that bread of life: he that cometh to me shall never hunger; and he that believeth on me shall never thirst.... I am that bread of life. Your fathers did eat manna in the wilderness, and are dead. This is the bread which cometh down from heaven, that a man may eat thereof, and not die. I am the living bread which came down from heaven: if any man eat of this bread, he shall live for ever: and the bread that I will give is my flesh, which I will give for the life of the world.... Verily, verily, I say unto you, Except ye eat the flesh of the Son of man, and drink his blood, ye have no life in you. Whoso eateth my flesh, and drinketh my blood, hath eternal life; and I will raise him up at the last day. For my flesh is meat indeed, and my blood is drink indeed" (John 6:32-55).

A final scripture is in Revelation 2:17 "...To him that overcometh will I give to eat of the hidden manna...." While we enjoy many revealed blessings of Christ and His Word, there remain many things which we do not yet understand. Because we do not understand them we must not deny them nor disbelieve them. If we remain faithful to the things we have and overcome through His blood and Word, the promise is that by and by we shall feast upon these hidden glories which will then be revealed.

"Take a pot, and put an omer full of manna therein, and lay it up before the Lord, to be kept for your generations. As the Lord commanded Moses, so Aaron laid it up before the Testimony, to be kept" (Ex. 16:33-34).

So it became part of the contents of the ark of God.

19

AARON'S ROD THAT BUDDED

Numbers 16 and 17.

"And the Lord spake unto Moses, saying, Speak unto the children of Israel, and take of every one of them a rod according to the house of their fathers, of all their princes according to the house of their fathers twelve rods: write thou every man's name upon his rod. And thou shalt write Aaron's name upon the rod of Levi: for one rod shall be for the head of the house of their fathers. And thou shalt lay them up in the tabernacle of the congregation before the testimony, where I will meet with you. And it shall come to pass, that the man's rod, whom I shall choose, shall blossom: and I will make to cease from me the murmurings of the children of Israel, whereby they murmur against you. And Moses spake unto the children of Israel, and every one of their princes gave him a rod apiece, for each prince one, according to their fathers' houses, even twelve rods: and the rod of Aaron was among their rods. And Moses laid up the rods before the Lord in the tabernacle of witness. And it came to pass, that on the morrow Moses went into the tabernacle of witness; and, behold, the rod of Aaron for the house of Levi was budded, and brought forth buds, and bloomed blossoms, and yielded almonds. And Moses brought out all the rods from before the Lord unto all the children of Israel: and they looked, and took every man his rod. And the Lord said unto Moses, Bring Aaron's rod again before the testimony, to be kept for a token against the rebels; and thou shalt quite take away their murmurings from me, that they die not. And Moses did so: as the Lord commanded him, so did he. And the children of Israel spake unto Moses, saying, Behold, we die, we perish, we all perish. Whosoever cometh any thing near unto the tabernacle of the Lord shall die: shall we be consumed with dying?" (Num. 17).

The third and final token found within the ark was the rod of Aaron that budded, blossomed, and brought forth almonds. This was the emblem of a God-chosen priesthood. **The Context.** The story, which occupies two chapters of the book of Numbers, tells of Korah, Dathan, and Abiram, who gathered together two hundred and fifty of the leading men of Israel in rebellion against Moses and Aaron. The accusation, which was a false one, was that Moses had overstepped the mark; he had usurped an authority, he was full of pride and, in calling in Aaron his brother as priest, had made a family concern of this leadership. The accusation stands in marked contrast to God's thought concerning Moses, which was: "Now the man Moses was very meek, above all the men which were upon the face of the earth" (Num. 12:3). Moses did the wisest thing it is possible to do when misjudged and misrepresented. He took it straight to the Lord.

God commanded that all the two hundred and fifty-three men should present themselves before Him the next day, and as they had asserted that they too could be priests they were to bring, each man, a priestly instrument, namely, a censer containing live fire and incense. After an exchange of accusations and reproof, God spoke. He declared that He would destroy the whole host, but Moses pleaded with God that they should not all die for one man's sin. God then bade the camp to separate themselves from the tents of the three leaders of the revolt, while Moses stood and addressed the assembly, saying: "Hereby ye shall know that the Lord hath sent me to do all these works; for I have not done them of mine own mind. If these men die the common death of all men, or if they be visited after the visitation of all men; then the Lord hath not sent me. But if the Lord make a new thing, and the earth open her mouth, and swallow them up, with all that appertain unto them, and they go down quick into the pit; then ye shall understand that these men have provoked the Lord" (Num. 16:28-30). Moses had barely finished this speech when the ground parted asunder and these men and their families were swallowed alive. What a picture of the proverb, "He, that being often reproved hardeneth his neck, shall suddenly be destroyed, and that without remedy" (Prov. 29:1). And what a fulfilment of "Heaven and earth shall pass away, but my words shall not pass away." These men were opposing the Word of God through Moses, but found the earth to slip from beneath their feet.

At the very time God was punishing the three men, a fire broke out and consumed the two hundred and fifty princes who had rebelled with them. From the burning embers the censers had to be rescued because they had been hallowed.

Instead of repenting the whole camp blamed Moses for the slaughter so that God's indignation was further increased, and the next day a plague broke out which would have destroyed all if Moses and Aaron had not stood between the living and the dead and made an atonement. The cost of that rebellion against the servants of the Lord was approximately fifteen thousand lives.

God then proceeded to give the people a further evidence of the fact that He had chosen Aaron as the High Priest, and so vindicated the characters of His servants.

The princes of the twelve tribes were each of them to bring a rod upon which Moses was to write their names. Moses was to present their rods before God by bringing them into the tabernacle and leaving them there overnight. The Lord said that the rod of the man He should choose should blossom. Next morning Moses went in to see the rods, and there he found one out of the twelve with buds, blossoms, and almonds upon it. The name on that rod was

Aaron, for the tribe of Levi. Every man was given back his rod; his name being on the rod prevented any discrepancy. The Lord then said: "Bring Aaron's rod again before the testimony, to be kept for a token against the rebels." The Apostle Paul, writing to the Hebrews, said that the rod was inside the ark, as also the pot of manna and the two tables of the covenant.

So much for the story concerning Aaron's rod, but now as to its meaning. It is clear from the foregoing that it represents a God-chosen priesthood. The evidences of such a priesthood are threefold. (1) Buds, the symbol of life. (2) Blossoms, the token of beauty. (3) Fruit, the sign of usefulness. There are three different priesthoods in Scripture which we will test by this God-given sign as to whether they are God-chosen.

1. Aaron Chosen Of God For Israel. The sign of the budding rod appears to have satisfied Israel. We never hear of them querying his right again after this. Perhaps the sign was a fit symbol of the life of Aaron.

Buds. Life came in a dead stick. The twelve rods laid up before the Lord were barren and had no contact with the earth, so the life that entered this one stick, causing it to bud, must have come from above. We feel sure that Aaron must have known something of a new life, a heaven-born life, or he would not have been chosen for such a position.

Blossom. God is the author of beauty. God looks for beauty of character, which is a gem in price far above rubies and diamonds. There was undoubtedly fragrance of character here, for God to choose this man.

Almonds. These betoken fruitfulness and wakefulness. Aaron must have been a man alert to responsibility and duty, a man upon whom God could depend.

In the natural the bud gives place to the flower, and the flower dies to make room for the fruit. But in this rod, Moses found it productive of all three at once. So it is in the spiritual realm. The Christian is never asked to forfeit the bud of new life, new joy, new love, new emotions. We are sometimes told to get back to our first love. Neither does a Christian have to discard beauty of character for usefulness in service.

2. Christ Chosen Of God For The Church. Christ claimed to be a priest of the Melchisedek order. Was He chosen of God, or did He take it upon Himself? If the sign of the rod satisfied Israel, it ought to satisfy us, so we will examine His life accordingly.

A Rod. This is what God used. This is what Christ was. The prophet said He was a root out of a dry ground; no form, no comeliness, no beauty to be desired. This "rod," like Aaron's, was presented with others before God. There were twelve all told with Aaron's rod, but only three when Christ was presented. He himself and two malefactors stood, or hung, before God, men, and devils. They all three died.

Bud. The third day life descended from above and entered into one of those three sticks, the one that bore the name of "priest," and He burst the bands of death and came forth into the newness of resurrection life. Up from the grave He arose!

Blossom. The fragrance of that resurrection life is seen in His post-resurrection movements, as He appeared here and there leaving wonderful words of cheer and hope to the crestfallen disciples whose hopes had been shattered by the death of their Lord a few days previously.

Almonds. The fruit of that resurrection life can be found in the words of the Lord as He says: "I am the firstfruits of them that sleep; as I live ye shall live also."

3. Believers Chosen Of God For The Unsaved. We, as believers, are priests and belong to a royal priesthood. Let us look for the symbol, and so see whether we are God-chosen.

A Rod. The Bible declares that there is none good, that we are dead in trespasses and in sins. In this condition we were brought into touch with Christ. We heard the way of salvation, we believed, and the result was:

Bud. Life came from above, entered into our dead souls, and we began to live. The life we now live we live by the faith of the Son of God. It is Christ dwelling in us. Therefore, there ought to be:

Blossom. Beauty of character, beauty of walk, beauty of holiness. Ours should be a life which, by its fragrance, should draw others to Christ. Our prayer and aim should be:

> "Let the beauty of Jesus be seen in me,
> All His wondrous compassion and purity.
> Oh! Thou Spirit Divine, all my nature refine,
> Till the beauty of Jesus be seen in me."

This will mean:

Almonds, or the life of fruitfulness. We ought to be bearing the fruit of the Spirit which is Love, Joy, Peace, Longsuffering, Gentleness, Goodness, Faith, Meekness and Self-control. This fruit should be ever increasing. According to John 15 it is fruit, more fruit, much fruit and fruit that remains.

If we, as priests, intercede with God, the fruit will be souls eternally saved, hearts continuously blessed, Christians constantly uplifted.

Chosen in Him.

20

THE JOURNEYINGS OF THE ARK

1. *From Sinai to Philistia*

Exodus 25 and 40. Numbers 3, 4, 10 and 14. Joshua
4, 6 and 7. 1 Samuel 2 and 4. Psalm 132.

"Lord, remember David, and all his afflictions: how he
sware unto the Lord, and vowed unto the mighty God of
Jacob; surely I will not come into the tabernacle of my house,
nor go up into my bed; I will not give sleep to mine eyes,
or slumber to mine eyelids, until I find out a place for the
Lord, an habitation for the mighty God of Jacob. Lo, we
heard of it at Ephratah: we found it in the fields of the wood.
We will go into his tabernacles: we will worship at his foot-
stool. Arise, O Lord, into thy rest; thou, and the ark of
thy strength. Let thy priests be clothed with righteousness;
and let thy saints shout for joy. For thy servant David's
sake turn not away the face of thine anointed. The Lord
hath sworn in truth unto David; he will not turn from it;
Of the fruit of thy body will I set upon thy throne. If thy
children will keep my covenant and my testimony that I
shall teach them, their children shall also sit upon thy throne
for evermore. For the Lord hath chosen Zion; he hath
desired it for his habitation. This is my rest for ever: here
will I dwell; for I have desired it. I will abundantly bless
her provision: I will satisfy her poor with bread. I will
also clothe her priests with salvation: and her saints shall
shout aloud for joy. There will I make the horn of David
to bud: I have ordained a lamp for mine anointed. His
enemies will I clothe with shame: but upon himself shall
his crown flourish" (Ps. 132).

We often hear the remark that the Old Testament is dry and uninteresting. That really depends upon the reader and how he approaches the Book. The story of the journeyings of the ark can be as thrilling and as exciting as any adventure story written in fiction. "Truth *is* stranger than fiction!"

The Ark of the Covenant carried with it the power of the God it represented. This power was from time to time manifested as it moved from place to place. But before we travel with it, it will be necssary to make one or two observations.

The psalm which precedes this chapter is one of the Songs of Degrees and was sung by the people as they journeyed with the ark before them. The ark was

Built At Sinai by Bezaleel and his workmen, who were skilled in all manner of cunning work because they were controlled by the Spirit of God. There is a thought just here. It is not the preacher and the minister only who need the Spirit of God resting upon them. God has promised His Spirit to all believers, so that it matters not what the nature of our service is we may know the help and guidance of the Holy Spirit. The ark did not become a sacred shrine until it was placed in the

Holy Of Holies. Then it was that the glory of the Shekinah presence of the Lord rested upon it. "And he brought the ark into the tabernacle, and set up the vail of the covering, and covered the ark of the testimony. . . . So Moses finished the work. Then a cloud covered the tent of the congregation and the glory of the Lord filled the tabernacle" (Ex. 40:21, 33, 34).

In all its journeyings the ark was

Carried By The Kohathites (Num. 3:30). They were one of the families of the tribe of Levi whose special burden was the ark, the candlestick, the table of shewbread, and the two altars, with all their vessels, and possibly the laver, but this is never mentioned.

Its Appearance (Num. 4:5, 6): "And when the camp setteth forward, Aaron shall come, and his sons, and they shall take down the covering vail, and cover the ark of testimony with it: and shall put thereon the covering of badgers' skins, and shall spread over it a cloth wholly of blue, and shall put in the staves thereof." All that the people saw, therefore, was a blue burden being borne upon the shoulders. This stood in contrast to all the other furniture, which was covered first by either a blue, purple, or scarlet cloth and afterwards, badgers' skins.

We now commence our travels.

The First Move (Num. 10:33): "And they departed from the mount of the Lord three days' journey: and the ark of the covenant of the Lord went before them in the three days' journey, to search out a resting place for them." Except for the next reference we shall consider, no more is said concerning the ark in all their forty years of traveling and wandering in the wilderness. This verse stands as an example. To put it again and again would only be unnecessary repetition. In this instance they journeyed three days. Sometimes they did more and sometimes they did less, but the ark always went before them. When the ark did set forward, Moses said: "Return, O Lord, unto the many thousands of Israel." This is the same ark as we have seen typifying Christ in all its construction. When we journey the Lord will go before us. He will keep us in all our ways, He will lead us by a right path; and when we rest it is He that make us to lie down in green pastures. We are able to say: "God is in the midst of us we shall not be moved."

This first example is to show us the joy of having God leading the way. The next and only other example in the wilderness is the reverse. What happens if He does not lead the way?

Absence Means Defeat (Num. 14:14). The camp had arrived at Kadesh-barnea. They had been safely brought across the wilderness. From here spies were sent ahead to spy out the land of Canaan, with the result that ten returned with an evil report and no evidence, and two returned with a good report and a tangible evidence that they were speaking the truth, for they brought with them a great cluster of grapes which they bore on their staff, and also pomegranates and figs. The people, with hearts full of doubt, ignored this practical demonstration and believed the words of the ten spies. They wept all night, and chided Moses and Aaron for bringing them to a place of death. The Lord's wrath was kindled against the people because this was the tenth time they had provoked Him and He said He would disinherit them; but once again Moses wonderfully prevailed with God in prayer and intercession. So instead of destroying them, He turned them southward, with their backs toward the promised land, into the the wilderness again, by way of the Red Sea, there to wander for forty years until all had died except Joshua and Caleb, the two worthy spies who, with a later generation, would enter the land. When God said: "Go up," they refused; now God is saying: "You shall not go up, but you shall perish in the wilderness," then they say: "We will go up." "And they rose up early in the morning, and gat them up into the top of the mountain, saying, Lo, we be here, and will go unto the place which the Lord hath promised: for we have sinned. And Moses said, Wherefore now do ye transgress the commandment of the Lord? but it shall not prosper. Go not up, for the Lord is not among you; that ye be not smitten before your enemies. . . . But they presumed to go up unto the hill top: nevertheless the ark of the covenant of the Lord, and Moses, departed not out of the camp. Then the Amalekites came down, and the Canaanites which dwelt in that hill, and smote them, and discomfited them, even unto Hormah" (Num. 14:40-45).

What lessons for us to learn! Firstly, rebellion and disobedience are disastrous and, secondly, if God is not with us, how helpless we are. We must always follow Christ and never go ahead of Him, or we will meet trouble.

The forty years have now expired and once more the children of Israel stand at the borders of the desired land. Between them and their promised possession is the swift current of the River Jordan. But the ark

Parts Jordan (Josh. 3 and 4). One stroke from the rod of Moses and God parted asunder the Red Sea, a type of salvation. But here at Jordan things are different. This time it was a step by step walk of faith.

The long-anticipated day had come. What a day of excitement! What a day of commands and instructions! What a day of obedience! They are not going to have a repetition of the evil day forty years previously. The officers commanded the people, saying: "When ye see the ark of the covenant of the Lord your God, and the priests the Levites bearing it, then ye shall remove from your place, and go after it." Then Joshua said to the priests: "Take up the ark of the covenant, and pass over before the people. And they took up the ark of the covenant, and went before the people." Then the priests came and stood with the ark on their shoulders, and put their feet in the water of the overflowing banks, while Joshua cried: "Behold, the ark of the covenant of the Lord of all the earth passeth over before you into Jordan." The priests proceeded into the waters of the Jordan and as they did the waters parted, and stood a great heap on either side. "And the priests that bare the ark of the covenant of the Lord stood firm on dry ground in the midst of Jordan, and all the Israelites passed over on dry ground, until all the people were passed clean over Jordan." Twelve chosen men followed and each took a stone from the bed of the river, where the priests had stood with the ark, and with the stones on their shoulders, went over to the other side. The priests came up following the twelve men, and as their feet touched the bank of the river so the waters returned to their place. The twelve stones were erected at Gilgal between Jordan and Jericho, where the people camped that night. They were now in the land.

Here we learn that whatever the obstacle, or however impossible the command of the Lord to us may appear, providing it is His command, He will see us safely through. Barriers must fall and problems melt before the presence of the "Ark" of our salvation.

While at Gilgal the Passover was observed, and the manna, hitherto so regularly given, now ceased. Then comes the next move forward. The ark

Takes Jericho (Josh. 6). Two spies had been into the city and rumor was current in Jericho that the Israelites were approaching. Travelers to the city had possibly brought news of the doings of these people and how they had crossed the Jordan. The city was, therefore, straitly shut up. Its walls were very formidable although not so formidable as the ten spies had once said, for they were a long way short of heaven and the citizens were not quite giants! Nevertheless, they had the advantage of the walls, a high position, and gates, whereas the Israelites had nothing — except *God,* and what an exception! He was a great Captain. The leader —Joshua — now issued the commands of the Captain. The Ark of the Covenant was to be carried around the city walls, preceded by seven priests with several trumpets and followed by all Israel's men of war. This was to be done once each day for six days, and on the seventh day they were to march around seven times. Throughout these marches the men were not allowed to speak a word. It was not to be what they thought, but what God had said that would bring them the victory. Then, with a blast of trumpets and a shout of triumph, down came the walls, out went the enemy, in went Israel. We must notice that the men shouted before the walls fell. It was a shout of faith.

We learned that God never removes the things that test our faith. Jericho had to be met even after forty years; but the Lord will give us the faith to stand the test if we let Him. Unfortunately, sin came into the camp through the disobedience of Achan. We now see that the ark

Humbles The Believer (Josh. 7:6): "And Joshua rent his clothes, and fell to the earth upon his face before the ark of the Lord until the eventide, he and the elders of Israel, and put dust upon their heads." God had done the previous work and had wrought for them a magnificent victory, but the men of Israel had endeavored to take to themselves the glory of it by estimating their own physical ability, quite leaving God out of the reckoning. "Let not all the people go up," say they, "but let about two or three thousand men go up and smite Ai; and make not all the people to labour thither; for they are but few." But instead of gaining the city they were defeated and lost thirty-six men. A Babylonian garment, two hundred shekels of silver and a wedge of gold, was the price for which their victory was sold. So Joshua stretched himself before the Lord in humility until God made known the reason. It was secret sin, and that only in one man. And more, the one man was not the leader but one of the rank and file. Has it ever occurred to you that a fault in one ordinary member of the church can rob the whole assembly of blessing, and bring spiritual defeat? So often when a church is not prospering, or any Christian work is failing to make advancement, we look to the minister or the leader for the cause. Maybe we ought to look to ourselves.

We now pass on to the time of Eli, the priest, and find the ark of God

At Shiloh (1 Sam. 1:3; 3:3). This was the permanent pitch of the tabernacle until the time when Solomon built the temple and the "curtains" were required no more. We are here introduced to the tabernacle set up within the land at a very dark time in Israel's history. Eli was old; his sons were not walking in the paths of righteousness, and there was no open vision. The word of the Lord was very precious in those days. But into the tabernacle had come a little boy consecrated to the Lord from his birth. His name was Samuel. "And ere the lamp of God went out in the temple of the Lord, where the ark of God was, and Samuel was laid down to sleep; that the Lord called Samuel: and he answered, Here am I." The Lord spoke to Samuel from off the mercy seat, and made known to him that which was to befall the house of Eli. The chapter following reveals to us that judgment, and in it the ark is taken

Prisoner Of War (1 Sam. 4). The first verse says: "Now Israel went out against the Philistines to battle. . . ." The children of Israel are in fault. If the Philistines had declared war, it might have been another matter. God had not told them to go, and it was very soon seen that they were out of the will of God for the battle went hard with them, four thousand being slain. They then thought of the ark of the Lord and said: "Let us fetch the ark of the covenant of the Lord out of Shiloh unto us, that, when it cometh among us, it may save us out of the hand of our enemies" (1 Sam. 4:3). So the ark was carried to the battlefield and when the soldiers saw it they raised a tremendous shout. As soon as the Philistines heard the shout they inquired the meaning of it, and when they heard that the ark of Israel's God had been brought, they were afraid, and the command was sent out: "Quit you like men, and fight as you have never fought before." The result was a great slaughter for Israel. Thirty thousand men were killed, including Hophni and Phinehas, the sons of Eli. Moreover, the Ark of the Covenant of the God of Israel was captured. Eli, the old priest, was sitting on a seat awaiting news of the battle, for his heart trembled for the safety of the ark. When the messenger came from the battlefield, he told Eli the sad story of defeat and how his two sons were killed and the ark taken. At the news of the capture of the ark the old man of ninety-eight fell from his seat and broke his neck. This now meant no priest, no successor to the priesthood, and no ark of God. While the battle went sore, and as Phinehas was killed, away back in the city his wife gave birth to a son. Upon hearing of the tragedies of the day and the loss of the ark and the priesthood, she named her newborn son, *Ichabod,* meaning "The glory of the Lord is departed."

Oh! What tragedies come through disobedience! Instead of the nation following the ark, they planned their attack, they made their arrangements, and then sought to bring the Lord into it as an afterthought, because things were difficult. Are we not often guilty of doing the same? We make our projects, we lay out our schemes for the running of a church, a mission, a campaign, this thing and that thing, and when we have done all, we call God in and ask Him to bless. May the dear Lord forgive us, and give us grace to follow Him and never ask Him to follow us, for it means utter failure and disappointment.

In the meantime, what happened to the ark? Did the enemy now possess the power of God to use it against His chosen people? Let us see in our next chapter.

21

THE JOURNEYINGS OF THE ARK

2. *From Philistia to the Temple*

1 Samuel 5, 6, and 7. 2 Samuel 6 and 7. 1 Kings 8:1-11.
2 Kings 24. Revelation 11:19.

"And it was told king David, saying, The Lord hath
blessed the house of Obed-edom, and all that pertaineth unto
him, because of the ark of God. So David went and brought
up the ark of God from the house of Obed-edom into the
city of David with gladness. And it was so, that when they
that bare the ark of the Lord had gone six paces, he sacri-
ficed oxen and fatlings. And David danced before the Lord
with all his might: and David was girded with a linen ephod.
So David and all the house of Israel brought up the ark of
the Lord with shouting, and with the sound of the trumpet.
And as the ark of the Lord came into the city of David,
Michal Saul's daughter looked through a window, and saw
king David leaping and dancing before the Lord; and she
despised him in her heart. And they brought in the ark of
the Lord, and set it in his place, in the midst of the tabernacle
that David had pitched for it: and David offered burnt-
offerings and peace-offerings before the Lord. And as soon
as David had made an end of offering burnt-offerings and
peace-offerings, he blessed the people in the name of the
Lord of hosts. And he dealt among all the people, even
among the whole multitude of Israel, as well to the women
as men, to every one a cake of bread, and a good piece of
flesh, and a flagon of wine. So all the people departed every
one to his house" (2 Sam. 6:12-19).

We closed the last chapter wondering what the Philistines would do with the ark and how they would fare with it in their possession. Well, they wondered too! We find they treated it with the greatest of reverence and brought it into the

House Of Dagon At Ashdod (1 Sam. 5:2), and set it beside their idol god. They did not know what else to do with it. To them the house was a holy place but to God it was an abomination, for Scripture declared that God and mammon cannot dwell together. Something must happen, and something did happen. Next morning Dagon was found lying on his face on the floor. This brought much consternation to the Philistines as carefully they put the idol back into its place, wondering how such an accident had happened. The day following they learned that it was more than an accident, for there lay their god on the ground again, but this time with both his head and his hands broken off. He was reduced to a torso. Being headless he could not think for them, see them or hear them, and having no hands he could not work for them. To the Philistines it must have been a great calamity. But we are reminded of the fact that the presence of God means the downfall of idolatry. Many people today have helpless idols which they worship, friends, habits, or possessions, that find first place in the life. When God comes in, in all the fullness of His power, these things go out as worthless. Verse 5 says: "Therefore neither the priests of Dagon, nor any that come into Dagon's house, tread on the threshold of Dagon in Ashdod unto this day."

The fall of Dagon was not the only strange thing that was happening, for a plague of emerods broke out in the city and many were dying. Therefore, they concluded that a curse was resting upon them and that the ark of the God of Israel was the cause; so they decided to send it away. It was taken to

Ashdod And Gath (1 Sam. 5). But in these two cities the same plague broke out and the hand of the Lord was very heavy against the men of these places. They therefore sent it away, and so it journeyed to

Ekron (1 Sam. 5:10). Here, too, people raised an objection to the very approach of the ark, saying: "They have brought about the ark of the God of Israel to us, to slay us and our people." The plague was so severe that it was called a "deadly destruction."

Having endured seven months' suffering, not being willing to part with the evidence of a great "victory," the hour of necessity came when the

Philistines Returned The Ark (1 Sam. 6). "But," said they, "send it not empty, nor alone, but send with it a trespass-offering that we may be healed." What could they send, for their worship differed from that of the Israelites? They decided, from their custom of giving to their god the representation of that from which they sought deliverance, to make five golden emerods and five golden mice, "images of your mice that mar the land." Here an inference is made to a further plague. Not only were the men smitten and Dagon overthrown, but the fields were also infested with field mice which were destroying the crops.

They had prepared their trespass offering but they had no priesthood to bare the ark back to his place, so they built a new cart. No doubt it was fear and awe that made them so careful. There came a hesitation in their purposes. Supposing after all it was not a plague inflicted by the God of Israel, but just a strange coincidence. They would "put out their fleece" and so we have the

Test Of The Milch Kine (1 Sam. 6). They took two milk cows, two mothers that were with their young. The young were penned up while the mothers were put into the cart with their heads turned toward Beth-shemesh where Israel was, and their backs turned on their young. If the cows went straight ahead with the ark, then the God of Israel has afflicted us, said the Philistines, but if the animals did what was the most natural thing for them to do, turn back when they heard the cry of their calves, then, said they, it was not God. This was an unfair and unnatural test. But God can stand tests even if they are unnatural, or contrary to nature. He is the God who had responded to Gideon with his fleece and, later, consumed with fire Elijih's saturated sacrifice. The glorious truth we behold in this incident is the willingness of God to return to a repentant people. If they will repent "I will heal their backsliding, I will love them freely..." (Hosea 14:4).

So the ark began its journey homeward, but it only arrived as far as

Beth-Shemesh (1 Sam. 6:19). The men of this city looked into the ark of the Lord. Whether out of concern for its entire safety, or whether out of idle curiosity, we do not know, but it was a tremendous sin of presumption, for in lifting the mercy seat they were lifting mercy from a law which they could not keep and so exposed themselves to the ministry of death. The result of that presumption was the death of 50,070 souls. The people of Beth-shemesh would have no more to do with the ark and sent messengers to the next town, Kirjath-jearim, saying: "The Philistines have brought again the ark of the Lord; come ye down, and fetch it up to you." So they came and carried the ark into the **House Of Abinadab In Kirjath-Jearim** (1 Sam. 7:1-2). The people of this place sanctified Eleazar, the son of Abinadab, to keep it. For twenty years did the ark remain here, during which time the house of Abinadab was greatly blessed. All homes that have Christ dwelling in them are homes of blessing.

Doing A Right Thing In A Wrong Way (2 Sam. 6). David then decided that he would have the ark brought up to Jerusalem. He gathered together thirty thousand chosen men and went down to Kirjath-jearim. The ark was put upon another new cart which was driven by the sons of Abinadab, and once more, after a score of years, the journey home was resumed. David and the people accompanied the ark playing on harps, psalteries, timbrels, cornets, and cymbals. All went well until they came to

Nachon's Threshingfloor (2 Sam. 6:6), where the ark toppled as the cart went over the rough floor, and Uzzah put forth his hand to steady the ark, and dropped dead. How did such a tragedy happen? God had instructed that staves should be put to the ark that it might be borne with them, and that it should be carried on the shoulders of the priests. It was in order for the Philistines to make a new cart, because they had no other means of conveying the ark. Had it been borne in the prescribed way it would never have tottered.

What are the lessons to be learned? First, that Christ, of whom the ark is a type, is to be borne upon the shoulders and in the lives of the believers, who are priests unto God. The reason why the church is in a condition of declension today is because men have been building their new carts, calling them new theology, modernism, higher criticism, and upon these carts they are seeking to fit Christ. The result has been a tottering and a falling in the church and some, like Uzzah, have had their faith destroyed as a result.

The second lesson comes from Uzzah whom some have sought to excuse and justify, but, in seeking to justify a person whom God has punished, one is charging God with injustice. If the ark was typical of Christ, and it was, then poor weak man was putting forth his hand to uphold a falling Christ. This seems a great statement to make; but in practice this is what many are doing today. The church is failing because it has put Christ onto carts of its own making, and to save it from failure, which men are attributing to the gospel instead of to themselves, they are seeking to support it by bridge parties, dances, films, etc. What a tragic story!

The result of this experience is that the journey is once more delayed and the ark is taken into the

House Of Obed-Edom (2 Sam. 6:10). There it remained for three months, while Obed-edom also received blessing. How true it is that, while many churches are losing blessing, individuals and small communities are enjoying great blessing. At the end of three months the ark is

Brought To Jerusalem (2 Sam. 6:12-19). This time it was carried in the correct way, on the shoulders of the priests, and with sacrifices and much national rejoicing. "And they brought in the ark of the Lord, and set it in his place, in the midst of the tabernacle that David had pitched for it: and David offered burnt-offerings and peace-offerings before the Lord." We must realize that this is the first time that the ark has been brought to Jerusalem. When it was taken as the spoil of warfare twenty-one years previously, its place was then in Shiloh. But having come to the capital city it is placed

In A Tent (2 Sam. 7:2). At this time every man had his home, and the king his palace. They were no more pilgrims and strangers, they were in the land. Yet the ark had no permanency yet. It reminds one of the days when Christ was here in the flesh, and we read concerning Him: "And every man went unto his own house. Jesus went unto the mount of Olives" (John 7:53; 8:1). There He spent the night. He had nowhere to lay His head. Men had their homes, but not Jesus. You, my reader, have your home. You go to it, you enjoy its comforts, its rest, its protection. Have you thought of where Christ is to dwell? His place is in your heart. He desires to dwell in you richly, but He will not come in unless He is invited.

A Temple Built (2 Sam. 7 and 1 Kings 5 to 8). David desired to build a place worthy of God, and so said to Nathan, the prophet: "See now, I dwell in an house of cedar, but the ark of God dwelleth in curtains." But God said: "Shalt thou build me an house for me to dwell in? Whereas I have not dwelt in any house since the time that I brought up the children of Israel out of Egypt, even to this day, but have walked with a tent and in a tabernacle." David was not permitted to build that house but God accepted the desire and promised that his son should build a house for His name. That temple was eventually built by Solomon. The day of dedication arrived and the ark was brought to its

Final Resting Place (1 Kings 8:1-8). "Then Solomon assembled the elders of Israel, and all the heads of the tribes, the chief of the fathers of the children of Israel, unto king Solomon in Jerusalem, that they might bring up the ark of the covenant of the Lord out of the city of David, which is Zion. And all the men of Israel assembled themselves unto king Solomon at the feast in the month Ethanim, which is the seventh month. And all the elders of Israel came, and the priests took up the ark. And they brought up the ark of the Lord, and the tabernacle of the congregation, and all the holy vessels that were in the tabernacle, even those did the priests and the Levites bring up. And king Solomon, and all the congregation of Israel, that were assembled unto him, were with him before the ark, sacrificing sheep and oxen, that could not be told nor numbered for multitude. And the priests brought in the ark of the covenant of the Lord unto his place, into the oracle of the house, to the most holy place, even under the wings of the cherubims. For the cherubims spread forth their two wings over the place of the ark, and the cherubims covered the ark and the staves thereof above. And they drew out the staves, that the ends of the staves were seen out in the holy place before the oracle, and they were not seen without: and there they are unto this day. There was nothing in the ark save the two tables of stone, which Moses put there at Horeb, when the Lord made a covenant with the children of Israel, when they came out of the land of Egypt. And it came to pass, when the priests were come out of the holy place, that the cloud filled the house of the Lord, so that the priests could not stand and minister because of the cloud: for the glory of the Lord had filled the house of the Lord."

There the ark remained in its dwelling place.

The Temple Destroyed (2 Kings 24 and 25). In the destruction of the temple and Jerusalem under the hand of Nebuchadnezzar and the carrying away into Babylon, much of the temple is referred to, but nothing is said concerning the ark. It is never seen nor heard of again. What became of it? We do not know. Some think it is hidden, others believe it will come to light again, but Jeremiah prophesying concerning Israel's future said: "And it shall come to pass, when ye be multiplied and increased in the land, in those days, saith the Lord, they shall say no more, the ark of the covenant of the Lord: neither shall it come to mind: neither shall they remember it; neither shall they visit it; neither shall that be done any more" (Jer. 3:16). This does not suggest a reappearance. I believe God in His own wonderful way removed that ark. We do not read, nor know anything, of its end. It has no end, so fulfilling its last and final type of Him who is eternal and who knows no end.

The ark has one more reference in Scripture.

The Ark In Heaven (Rev. 11:19). "And the temple of God was opened in heaven, and there was seen in his temple the ark of his testament." "See that thou make it according to the pattern shown thee in the mount," was the instruction given to Moses. Here is the pattern. In type and in shadow we have meditated upon Christ and His Church. When we get to the "It is finished" of life and arrive in the glory land, we shall behold the "It is finished" of our salvation. For that ark is Christ!